CU00894792

LILLIAN T
JENNIFE
2012
FORTUNE &
FENG SHUI
RABBIT

KONSEPBOOKS
ASTROLOGY . FENG SHUI . INSPIRATIONS

Congratulations!

Hi there!

Firstly, I want to thank and congratulate you for investing in yourself… and the latest edition of Fortune and Feng Shui… your personalized horoscope book for 2012! Today you have purchased one of the best possible books on the market today to guide and help you safely through the upcoming year!

What will you be earning one year from today? How will you look and feel… will you be happier and healthier in 2012?

In this little book, Jennifer and I reveal many insights pertaining to your particular animal sign…what you can expect and how to protect and enhance all areas of your life for success in 2012.

But Why Stop Here?

Now you can discover other powerful feng shui secrets from me that go hand-in-hand with the valuable information in this book. And it's absolutely FREE!

My Personal Invitation

I'd like to extend my personal invitation to you to receive my FREE online weekly newsletter... Lillian Too's Mandala Ezine. You took the first positive step to success when you purchased this book. Now you can expand your wealth luck and knowledge...and learn more about authentic feng shui that really works... including the all-important 3rd dimension of spiritual feng shui when you sign up for my FREE newsletter.

Just go to *www.liliantoomandalaezine.com* and register today! My ezine will be delivered to your inbox each week loaded with great feng shui articles, hints and tips to make 2012 your best year ever.

IT'S EASY! IT'S FREE! IT'S FRESH AND NEW EACH WEEK!

Don't miss out! It's easy to register at *www.lilliantoomandalaezine.com* and you'll also receive a special BONUS from me when you register today!

All the best,
Lillian

P.S. Lillian's online FREE weekly ezine is only available to those who register online at *www.lilliantoomandalaezine.com*

P.P.S. Ezine subscribers also receive special offer, discounts and bonuses from me throughout the year!

Fortune & Feng Shui 2012 RABBIT
by Lillian Too and Jennifer Too
© 2012 Konsep Lagenda Sdn Bhd

Text © 2012 Lillian Too and Jennifer Too
Photographs and illustrations © WOFS.com Sdn Bhd

The moral right of the authors to be identified as authors of this book has
been asserted.

Published by KONSEP LAGENDA SDN BHD (223 855)
Kuala Lumpur 59100 Malaysia

For more Konsep books, go to www.lillian-too.com or www.wofs.com
To report errors, please send a note to errors@konsepbooks.com
For general feedback, email feedback@konsepbooks.com

ISBN 978-967-329-073-4
Published in Malaysia, August 2011

for more on all the recommended
feng shui cures, remedies & enhancers for

2012

please log on to

www.wofs.com

and

www.fsmegamall.com

RABBIT BORN CHART

BIRTH YEAR	WESTERN CALENDAR DATES	AGE	KUA NUMBER MALES	KUA NUMBER FEMALES
Earth Rabbit	19 Feb 1939 to 7 Feb 1940	73	7 West Group	8 West Group
Metal Rabbit	6 Feb 1951 to 26 Jan 1952	61	4 East Group	2 West Group
Water Rabbit	25 Jan 1963 to 12 Feb 1964	49	1 East Group	5 West Group
Wood Rabbit	11 Feb 1975 to 30 Jan 1976	37	7 West Group	8 West Group
Fire Rabbit	29 Jan 1987 to 16 Feb 1988	25	4 East Group	2 West Group
Earth Rabbit	16 Feb 1999 to 4 Feb 2000	13	1 East Group	5 West Group

CONTENT

CHAPTER 1.
Dragon Year 2012 - General Outlook

Transformational Energies
Bring a Year of Far-reaching Changes   12

- The Year's Dominant Energies   12
- General Outlook for the year   20
- The PAHT CHEE chart of 2012   24
- Influence of the PAHT CHEE "stars"   32
- The FLYING STAR Numbers of 2012   38
- The "luck stars" of the 24 mountains   55

CHAPTER 2.
Luck Of The Rabbit In 2012

Fortune Prospects & Energy Strength   73

- Outlook for Lady RABBIT   82
- Outlook for Gentleman RABBIT   86
- Energy Strength analyses of RABBIT luck in 2012   89
- RABBIT's Life Force and Health Luck   89
- RABBIT's Finance and Success Luck   91
- RABBIT's Chi Essence   94
- Metal Rabbit – 61 years – Excellent Year. Happiness.   95
- Water Rabbit – 49 years – Stable but exciting   96
- Wood Rabbit – 37 years – So good   96
- Fire Rabbit – 25 years – Chances turn sour with impatience 97
- Earth Rabbit – 73 & 13 years – Everything going swell   97

CHAPTER 3.
Personalising Your Feng Shui Luck In 2012

Individualised Directions to Protect Your Good Feng Shui

98

- Making RABBIT's East location auspicious   101
- Enhancing RABBIT's Personal Kua Numbers   104
- Fine-tuning Auspicious Directions for RABBIT women   108
- Fine-tuning Auspicious Directions for RABBIT men   110
- Important pointers for work, health, study luck & relationships   111

CHAPTER 4.
Relationship Luck For 2012

Your strength is appreciated by those who come into contact with you

122

- **Rabbit With Rabbit** – Generating warm feelings   136
- **Rabbit With Sheep** – Competitive feelings cause jealousy   138
- **Rabbit With Boar** – Enhancing each other's performance   141
- **Rabbit With Dog** – There is mistrust between this pair   146
- **Rabbit With Tiger** – Synergy Luck generates warm feelings   148
- **Rabbit With Rooster** – Surprisingly cordial in a great year   154
- **Rabbit With Rat** – Staying true despite distractions   157
- **Rabbit With Ox** – Excellent luck for this pair   160
- **Rabbit With Dragon** – Environmentally friendly couple   163
- **Rabbit With Snake** – Hostile sparks fly   165
- **Rabbit With Horse** – Too much loving here   168
- **Rabbit With Monkey** – Not good for each other   170

CHAPTER 5.
Analysing Your Luck In Each Month

**Many months of the year favor you;
but it is vital not to loosen your guard**   172

February 2012 – A quarrelsome start causes tensions   173

March 2012 – Illness and a weak body take their toll   176

April 2012 – Come spring time and you are reenergised   179

May 2012 – Good month when everything starts to happen   182

June 2012 – Sheer brilliance lighting up your life   185

July 2012 – Overconfidence can make you careless   188

August 2012 – Sum-of-Ten brings very positive luck   191

September 2012 – Troubles on the domestic front   194

October 2012 – Too much loving cause costly distractions   197

November 2012 – Hostility in personal life   200

December 2012 – Chill out to escape sickly blues   203

January 2013 – Time to begin another brand new year   206

CHAPTER 6.
Powerful Protection With Tien Ti Ren

Activating The Complete Trinity Of Luck With Spiritual Feng Shui

Activating The Complete Trinity Of Luck With Spiritual Feng Shui   209

- **Special Incense Offerings** to appease local guardian spirits   216
- **Customized Amulet** to add to Rabbit's strong success elements   220
- **Clear Crystal Ball** to bring Rabbit to new power level   223
- **Wish-Granting Gem Tree** wealth creation luck   224
- **Golden Power Wheel** Powerful symbol of Upward Mobility   226
- **Plaque of Blue Dragon Ascending to Heaven**   227
- **Fire Totem Talisman Pendant** to safeguard longterm luck   228
- **Guardian Bodhisattva** - Invoking Rabbit's Guardian   230

YEAR OF THE WATER DRAGON 2012
A Transformational Year

The Rabbit-born discards the tribulations and setbacks of the past year and emerges strong, steady and very clued-on in 2012. In this new year of the Water Dragon, many things happening in the world are colored by the powerful presence and strength of the Dragon, the Zodiac system's most powerful sign.

The year 2012 is going to be a transformational year with Dragon energy permeating both positive and negative manifestations of luck and the Rabbit-born is all set to make the most of the year's favorable and loving energy.

This coming year, the stars and element distribution of the annual paht chee chart bring early indications of far-reaching and life-changing developments. For those born in the year of the Rabbit, the feng shui winds of Dragon energy are quite excellent indeed. These indicate new relationships coming into your life. What is great is that for many of you, your enthusiasm and verve allow you to rise to the challenge of making many good things happen for you.

But Rabbits, like everyone else, must cope with the stars (good as well as bad) affecting the year.

First, note the 3 stars influencing the energy of the year.

The Star of Aggressive Sword makes an appearance, so there is a great need to be wary. Violence in the world has not yet abated. There continues to be an air of anger pervading the world's atmosphere, a collective anger that continues to find an outlet.

Interestingly also, in the 2012 paht chee chart, the Tiger continues to be around and it is a **strong Water Tiger** that complements the year's **Water Dragon**. With Tiger and Dragon present in the chart, and the Rooster as well (which symbolizes the Phoenix and is the Dragon's secret friend), we see the presence of three celestial guardians as well as the powerful hand of heaven. It is a year when destinies play out with brutal efficiency and big transformations take place. This is confirmed by the number 6 in the center of the feng shui chart. Heavenly energies rule this year.

Cosmic forces are extremely powerful in 2012 and the best way to ride the Dragon year, the most effective way to emerge stronger and healthier, happier and richer, is to rely greatly on powerful cosmic guardians. And to always wear symbols of victory! Protection and enhancers are important aids to riding the Dragon in 2012. It is also beneficial to learn subduing rituals that ward off bad luck vibes bringing violence. It is a year when wearing protective powerful mantras and syllables on the body can mean the difference between sailing through the year safely or becoming some kind of victim.

Put on protective amulets that touch the energy vortexes of your throat, your heart and near to the navel where your body's central chakra is located, and where all the "winds" of the body's channels converge.

Strengthening the chakras of the human body system enhances attunement to the environment. We are currently living through a time when the energies of the world are in a state of flux. Staying protected and in sync with the disturbing energies of the environment is not difficult and is worth the small effort involved.

The year 2012 also brings the Star of the *External Flower of Romance*, a star which fuels potentially painful passions. Those hit by it and engage in affairs out of wedlock are certain to create hurtful waves and aggravations in their lives! Relationship woes could well escalate in 2012; it will be worse than last year and no one is immune!

> It is wise to take some strong precautions. Bring good feng shui protection into the bedroom and be particularly conscious of **auspicious sleeping directions** that protect the family and your marriage relationship this year. Also put into place safeguards that protect your particular love relationship.

For the ambitious and for those determined to succeed, the year also brings the *Star of Powerful Mentors*. For the younger generation of Rabbit, and especially those whose birth charts have the vital Fire element (which is missing this year), there is the auspicious luck of influential people turning up in their lives to give them strong and meaningful support.

This applies to those born with Fire in the heavenly stem of their year pillars, so the **25 year old Rabbit born** will benefit from the authority and mentor figures in their lives. Knowing about the presence of the *Mentor Star* in the year's chart should make you be on the lookout for potential mentors who can help and guide you through your professional life. These figures of influence are sure to open doors to better opportunities and help you along your path up the career ladder. The presence of the Fire element in your chart is a good indication. It suggests a better balanced set of energies that is in good sync with the year. There will be unseen hands supporting you.

Compass directions and locations of sleeping areas must be correctly monitored this year; and the symbol of the **Crystal Globe with Dragon** perched at the top ascending towards the Universe and the skies attracts all-important heaven luck.

We have designed a very special crystal globe to be placed in the center of homes especially for this purpose - to act as a catalyst. This Dragon sitting on top of the crystal globe adds much towards enhancing the energy of the Rabbit's home.

The Crystal Globe with Dragon attracts Heaven Luck and enhances the center number of the Flying Star Chart of the year, the Heavenly 6.

It is also a year to take note of the luck of different months so that your luck is properly fine-tuned. Be on the lookout for your good months, for these are times when you can be confident, and when opportunities will ripen in an auspicious manner. Troubled months are when it is advisable to refrain from making big decisions or embarking on important journeys; they are also the times to put suitable remedies in place so that whatever setbacks, illness or disappointments you have to face will be minor in nature.

This series of *Fortune & Feng Shui books* for the twelve animal signs of the Lunar Zodiac is written based on studies made into the year's Paht Chee and feng shui charts. Information in these charts are combined with Flying Star Feng Shui, the 24 Mountains Compass Stars Cycle and the Tibetan Wheel of Elements, to bring you accurate readings on what to expect for the coming year.

We go to great lengths to analyze the charts and research the cures so that we can incorporate powerful feng shui and astrological recommendations. Our philosophy of practice is that bad luck should always be effectively averted and good luck must always be strongly activated to manifest. So these books are not mere passive readings of luck. This year we focus on the importance of house layout design and feng shui directions, as these appear to offer the best ways of taking fullest advantage of the Dragon, Tiger and Phoenix celestial presence in the paht chee chart. This is an auspicious configuration which has the potential to channel heavenly good fortune your way. So included within is advice about placement of symbolic objects that have a celestial connection. Placed correctly within the home, they act as catalysts to luck, thus facilitating your journey through the year ensuring you sail through relatively trouble-free.

The big thing for 2012 is **the power of the Blue Dragon** and the **great importance of Fire energy**, because Fire is missing in this year's chart. The presence of Fire will instantly improve the luck of any space. This is a year to invest in **bright lights and candles**.

The presence of **crystal/glass globes** and **wish granting jewels** in the center of the home will also be especially auspicious, as this brings the **luck of increasing wealth.** In 2012 the element that signifies prosperity is the **Earth element**, so having crystal balls on your coffee tables, especially those embellished with auspicious syllables and prosperity sutras, are sure to offer excellent harmonious relationship luck.

These books are meant to assist readers to understand **how their astrological and destiny luck can be improved with good feng shui** in this important transformational year of the Dragon. Recommendations are based on calculations and interpretations of the charts, and analysis has been simplified so that the advice given is easily understood. Even those with no previous experience with feng shui or fortune enhancement practices will find it easy, fun and **ultimately very effective** using astrology and the placement of symbolic objects to improve their luck.

This book on the Rabbit's fortunes for 2012 is one of twelve written specially for each Zodiac sign. It offers almost a recipe-type easy approach to preparing for the year ahead. If you find it helpful for yourself, you might also want to monitor the luck pattern of your loved ones. Who knows how good advice given within may be just the thing to jump-start their auspicious fortune, causing it to ripen! In this Year of the Dragon, everything good or bad will seem to be larger than usual in magnitude and definitely transformational in effect. It is worthwhile taking some trouble to ensure that the year's energy syncs beautifully with yours.

GENERAL OUTLOOK FOR THE YEAR

There were severe earthquakes, floods, storms, forest fires and volcanic eruptions in the past two years, creating a disaster-driven scenario which last year was compounded by the severity of violence and civil conflicts in many of the world's troubled countries.

The last two years 2010 and 2011 saw troubled times brought by the clash of stem and branch elements, not just in the important year pillar, but also in all the other pillars.

These paht chee chart indications brought suffering and loss on a global scale, and in the immediate past year, they manifested in different parts of the world with frightening reality.

The violence that erupted in the countries of Northern Africa and the Middle East were scary but so were city shattering earthquakes, widespread floods, gigantic storms, volcanic eruptions and terrifying tsunamis, all of which started towards the closing months of 2010 and continuing into 2011. These seem to lend credence to the highly publicized end-of-world predictions for 2012.

Yet happily, amidst all the natural disasters and violence that have occurred, those who stayed safe also went on to enjoy good times and good news. This was because the year 2011 also benefited from powerful feng shui winds and enjoyed windows of good fortune brought by quite a good number of big and small auspicious star energies from the 24 mountain compass stars.

Unfortunately you, the Rabbit, were afflicted by the Five Yellow last year, so it is unlikely you benefited as much as some of the other signs, but you can more than make up for it this year, as the elements and energy winds of 2012 do favor you strongly.

Basically, the destiny chart of elements of the past couple of years did bring turbulent times and conflicts to many parts of the world, but these discordant energies told only half the story. On a micro basis, many were able to seize the opportunities that manifested during the past year. For 2012, Chinese Astrology does not predict an end of world scenario. But will we see an end to the disaster scenario of the past two years? The charts suggest a slowing down.

2012 is the Year of the powerful Water Dragon, and the astrological indications of the year are predicting a transformational year. There are absolutely no signs of the physical world coming to an end, but the charts do point to a time of great upheaval brought about by the disasters of past years and also rather awesome change - when the world as we know it continues on a path of transformation started two years ago, and gathering momentum in 2012.

These changes, which are political as well as economic, will impact the lives of many people and change the balance of influence and power in the world. But the good news is that it is also a year of renewal - at least the beginnings of good times ahead - of seeing the light at the end of the tunnel.

The Dragon Year always symbolizes an apex of change. It is the celestial creature of Spring, so a year ruled by the Dragon is always a time when the world will experience new beginnings in multiple dimensions of existence. The 2012 Dragon will see many countries changing directions in terms of allegiances and economic emphasis. New leaders will also emerge and violence could precede or follow upon such change.

Commercially, the world becomes more competitive and demanding. Relationships are edgy and there is an absence of general goodwill. This is due to the preponderance of *yearly conflict stars*. And there is also the *influential Aggressive Star* hanging over the year's paht chee.

So although natural disasters and severe fallouts caused by weather changes reduce in severity, human conflicts continue to escalate. Tolerance amongst world leaders is almost nonexistent so we shall hear the rattling of threats and the smell of war. This is compounded by the clashing elements in the year pillar of the Dragon - when Earth clashes with Water - so conflicts do not get resolved.

Happily for mankind, this is not a fierce clash. Here, it is Earth stabilizing Water rather than Metal destroying Wood. Besides, it is a year when the presence of the *lap chun* brings the promise of potentially good growth.

When growth energy is as strong as it is in this new year, it brings a good harvest, so symbolically, this is an encouraging sign. Also, there is ONE pillar of the paht chee chart that shows a productive relationship between the elements, that of **Yang Water** producing **Yang Wood** in the Month pillar. This gives hope of rejuvenation.

The year also sees the heavenly lucky 6 in the center of the feng shui chart & this brings auspicious luck from above. Engaging the energy of *tien* or heaven is the key to staying in perfect sync with the year and is what will unlock good fortune luck. This involves inviting cosmic Deities into the home.

This is also a year blessed by the presence of three celestial creatures - **the Dragon, Tiger and Phoenix** (the presence of the Rooster in the year's chart signifies the phoenix) and these bring very welcome powerful and protective energies. Astrologically therefore, this is a much better year than last in terms of planting new growth and reaping good harvests. The energies of the Dragon Year are conducive to new ideas and new ways of improving oneself. Investments can be made on healthy foundations, and prosperity can be nurtured.

THE PAHT CHEE CHART OF 2012

The Four Pillars chart of 2012 reveals not just the general trends of the year, but also gives a helicopter view of what can be expected in terms of trends and opportunities. The chart comprises a basket of eight elements that influences the luck of the year.

The composition of this basket of elements - Fire, Earth, Metal, Water and Wood - and the frequency of the appearance of each in the chart is what shows us what elements are missing, which are in short supply and which are in excess. We also analyze the chart to determine the stability of the year's energies and we go deeper to look for hidden elements that bring additional inputs to the year.

HOUR	DAY	MONTH	YEAR
HEAVENLY STEM	HEAVENLY STEM	HEAVENLY STEM	HEAVENLY STEM
乙	乙	壬	壬
YIN WOOD	YIN WOOD	YANG WATER	YANG WATER
EARTHLY BRANCH	EARTHLY BRANCH	EARTHLY BRANCH	EARTHLY BRANCH
辛 酉	己 未	甲 寅	戊 辰
METAL ROOSTER	EARTH SHEEP	WOOD TIGER	EARTH DRAGON

HIDDEN HEAVENLY STEMS OF THE YEAR

-	YIN WOOD YIN FIRE	YANG EARTH YANG FIRE	YIN WATER YIN WOOD

THE YEAR IS DESPERATELY SHORT OF FIRE IE INTELLIGENCE & CREATIVITY

The 2012 chart has only four of the five elements, so it is incomplete - there is one element missing. **The missing element is FIRE** which instantly suggests to anyone who understands the vital importance of balancing the elements that everyone's home will benefit from extra lighting during the coming Dragon year. Keeping the home well lit instantly enhances the energies of any home, bringing a more auspicious foundation for the year.

It is beneficial to install **more lights**, to keep curtains to a minimum and to literally bring the sunshine in. The **Fire** element in 2012 **signifies intelligence and creativity**, and there is a shortage of this during the year, so bringing well thought out ideas to any situation improves the success equation.

It is the clever and the wise that will ultimately prevail this year. So curb your impulses and always think things through before making important decisions. Happily, there are two hidden Fire elements in the chart, and this makes up for the lack of Fire in the main chart. This is a good sign, but hidden Fire can also mean Fire erupting, so there will continue to be calamities associated with hidden Fire.

Meanwhile, looking deeper into the chart, we see that there is more than enough Wood and Water energy in 2012. In fact, Wood energy is very strong, and could even be too strong. This suggests a degree of competitiveness that can turn ugly; excess Wood makes everyone more combative and scheming than usual. Neither friends nor allies are particularly helpful to each other. The hard-line impulses of the year's energies tend to be pervasive, so for the next twelve months, it is a case of **every man for himself** being the rallying cry.

> There is also **very serious jostling for power** and rank in many people's lives. Especially amongst leaders, people in charge, and those who supervise others… their motivation will mainly be to outdo and outperform whoever is identified as the challenger. Success this year has to be achieved against this **very competitive scenario**. It plays out on any scale, macro or micro, from the smallest office situation to the global world stage; in the playing fields or in the workplace.

The energy of the working world tends to be antagonistic and hostile, fueled by the presence of the *Aggressive Star*. Words spoken will be louder and more forceful and especially between those at the

27

top. Amongst patriarchal people, many will tend to be extra territorial, more assertive and very definitely more uncompromising. This attitude of belligerence will be the main obstacle to harmony this year.

Amongst the four pillars of the chart, you can see that three of them have clashing elements.

In the Year pillar, the heavenly stem of Yang Water clashes with the Earthly branch of Yang Earth. Here the heavenly stem energy is subdued by the earthly branch. The Dragon's earthly influence will be strong.

In the Day pillar, the heavenly stem of Yin Wood destroys the Earthly branch of Yin Earth. Here, the heavenly stem prevails. The Sheep essence here is subdued by heavenly energy.

In the Hour pillar, the heavenly stem of Yin Wood is destroyed by the Earthly branch of Yin Metal. We see here the earthly strength of the Rooster.

With 3 out of 4 of the pillars clashing, the year will not be peaceful. Harmony is a hard commodity to come by. But note that **in the Month pillar** Yang Water enhances Yang Wood. This is very auspicious as this means there is implied growth energy during the year.

WEALTH LUCK IN 2012 is signified by the element of Earth and with two of these in the main chart as well as one hidden Earth element, there is wealth luck during the year. It should not be difficult for wealth luck to manifest or to get enhanced. What is great is that in the hidden elements of this Month pillar, we see the presence of Fire enhancing Earth. This is a good sign and since it is the Month pillar, it benefits those who undertake wealth-enhancing activities during the months that are favorable for them. So do make an effort to remember your lucky months during the course of the year. Getting your timing right is often the key to making good decisions.

For the Rabbit, the lucky months for engaging in prosperity-enhancing activities are **June & August**, i.e. during the summer months, and also in **January of 2013** when projects you work on come to a good conclusion. These are the months when you will benefit from auspicious luck coming your way.

RESOURCE LUCK IN 2012 is represented by the element of Water. There are two direct Water and one hidden Water in the chart and once again, this is a good sign as it means there will be enough resources to keep the year's growth energy stable and strong. In paht chee

29

readings, emphasis is always placed on the stability of good luck manifesting.

This year, Water ensures that the intrinsic Wood energy of the year is kept constantly nourished. The resource availability situation appears good. This also suggests that the price of oil will not be so high as to cause problems to world economic growth.

> The **main danger** is that there might be excess Water. Too much Water can create an imbalance, in which case it should be balanced by the presence of Fire energy.

The clever balancing of elements in your living space is the key to attracting and sustaining good fortune, so make an effort to increase the presence of Fire energy in your living and working spaces. Use red scatter cushions and red curtains, and enhance your lighting this year!

POWER LUCK IN 2012 is represented by the element of Metal and in the chart there is one occurrence of Metal represented by the earthly branch of the Rooster sign. That there is only a single occurrence of Metal suggests however that power luck in 2012 is not strong; that it is in the Hour pillar means power chi comes more towards the end of the year, and power this year is held by the young person.

> The year favors power that is exercised by the **younger generation** of the family, and more effective when wielded by **females**.

What is very encouraging is that the Rooster and Dragon are *Secret Friends* of the Astrological Zodiac. The presence of this auspicious pair of celestial creatures in the year's Paht Chee bodes well for the beginning and end of the year. Their joint presence also subdues to some extent the conflict energy of the year.

The presence of the 3 celestial protectors - the Dragon, Phoenix and Tiger appearing together in the chart is also another good indication. These are three of the four celestial guardians of any space. They signify that **protector energy** is present during the year and to make the energy complete, it is very beneficial in 2012 to invite in the celestial Tortoise.

In 2012, all homes benefit from the presence of the **Celestial Tortoise**. Inviting an image of the tortoise into the home is beneficial and timely.

Better yet is to start keeping some live tortoises or terrapins. Doing so completes the powerful quartet of celestial guardians in your home.

Influence of the Paht Chee Stars

In 2012, we see the presence of three powerful stars in the Paht Chee chart. These bring additional dimensions to the year's outlook. They define the attitudes that have a dominant influence on people's tendencies and behavior. The three stars are:

- ▶ the Star of Aggressive Sword
- ▶ the Flower of External Romance
- ▶ the Star of Powerful Mentors

Star of Aggresive Sword

This star suggests a year of intensive aggression. It indicates the strengthening of the underdog's chi energy, so it does point to a continuation of the revolutionary energies started last year. Across the globe, there will be a rise of revolutionary fervor; people revolting against established authority.

At its zenith, the presence of this star suggests the emergence of powerful rebel leaders, or of highly influential opposition to established leaders. It suggests the emergence of people who seize power by fair means or foul. The name of this star is *Yang Ren*, which describes **yang essence sharp blade that inflicts damage**. This is a star that has great potential for either very good or very bad influences to materialize during the year, although generally, the influence tends to be more negative than positive. Unfortunately in the chart of this year, the Star of Aggressive Sword is created by the strong Yin Wood of the Day Pillar with the presence of the Tiger in the Month pillar.

Here, note that the Wood element is strong in the chart, making the presence of the **Aggressive Sword Star** much more negative. It indicates that those emerging as leaders for the underdog in 2012 will end up being heavy-handed and quick tempered.

They are charismatic but will also be strong-willed, conceited , arrogant, overbearing and self centered - all negative traits that spell the potential for bloodshed and violence wherever they emerge. This is a real danger for the year!

CURE: In case you need protection against being personally hit by the influence of the **Star of Aggressive Sword,** or if you live inww a part of the world where revolution has already just occurred or where there has been a recent change of Government or where violence prevails, you will need the powerful **Earth Stupa of Protection.** This brass stupa is filled with powerful **Dharmakaya Relic mantras** within and has a protective amulet on its façade which specifically protects against dangers of any kind of violence around you.

The Earth Stupa of Protection is the best cure to use to stay protected against the Star of Aggressive Sword this year.

Flower of Romance (External)

The *Flower of Romance* is sometimes confused with the *Peach Blossom Star* because it addresses the subject of love. When the flower of romance is present in the Eight Characters chart, it suggests that there is genuine love and caring between husband and wife.

But this is a star that also **reveals the occurrence of extramarital affairs**. The differentiation is made between internal romance and external romance, with the latter implying the occurrence of infidelity.

The **Flower of Romance Star** indicated in this year's chart is that of **external romance**, so it suggests the **occurrence of infidelity** within long term love relationships, causing problems and heartaches. Marriages suffer the dangers that this year's flower of romance star poses. It is thus really helpful to wear or display the safeguards that protect the sanctity of love relationships.

In 2012 the *External Flower of Romance* is created by the earthly branch Dragon in the Year pillar and the earthly branch Rooster in the Hour pillar.

CURE: To combat this serious affliction during the year, those of you worried about infidelity in your marriage or have cause to suspect your partner of harboring thoughts of infidelity, we suggest you either wear the **amulet which protects against third party interference** in your relationship (and this is very powerful) OR you can also invite in the **image of a Dog & Rabbit** to counter the affliction. This subdues the possibility of infidelity causing problems for you. The Dog/Rabbit presence will create a special "cross" with the Dragon/Rooster affliction in the year's chart.

Star of Powerful Mentors

Chinese Astrology makes much of "mentor" luck, and in the old days, having a powerful patron looking after your career path at the Emperor's court was an important success factor. The prospects facing young scholars hoping to rise to powerful positions at the Court of the Emperor was always enhanced with the help of someone influential.

In modern times, it is just as excellent to enjoy the luck of being supported, helped and guided by powerful benefactors. Indeed, success often comes from "who you know rather than what you know."

In 2012, the presence of the **Star of Powerful Mentors** emphasizes the importance of Mentor Luck, so that **those having someone powerful** to help them in their professional or business career **will have the edge** in terms of attaining success.

ENHANCER: To attract Mentor Luck into your life, display a large statue of **Kuan Kung, the God of Advancement and Wealth**, in the front part of the home or in the Northwest corner of the home. The presence of this proud Taoist Deity is believed to attract into the home the **powerful support** of a patriarchal figure that will bring good influence to the lives of those about to embark on a career. Kuan Kung also **protects against violence** that may harm the patriarch!

Kuan Kung, the God of Advancement and Wealth, enhances the Star of Powerful Mentors. Invite him into your home to ensure you get all the help that you need to achieve success this year.

37

THE FLYING STAR NUMBERS OF 2012

The Flying Stars chart of 2012 is dominated by the auspicious *Heavenly Star* number 6 in the center. This is a strong star. It brings a multi-dimensional manifestation of unexpected good fortune, especially when it gets activated. Activating any good flying star in any year is part of practising time dimension feng shui. There are three effective ways of putting this energy to work for you, all three of which are done with the intention of attracting yang chi into the part of the home which houses the auspicious star number, in this case the number 6 in the center of the home or the center of any room.

The three methods of activating yang chi are:

Firstly, create noise...
with a radio or television placed here in the center.

Secondly, create activity...
by having a sitting arrangement here. Human energy is most powerful in activating the chi.

Thirdly, create light...
place a bright light in the place where the 6 is located. In 2012, this has a double benefit, as Fire

energy, represented by light, is what brings excellent balancing feng shui.

When energized in any of these three ways, the number 6 will be activated to bring good energies into the home. It is also possible to enhance this star number further by placing powerful **Earth element energy** here in the center of the home. Earth element magnifies the power of metallic 6, so having **crystal or glass balls** on a coffee table in the center of your living room area would be most auspicious indeed. The best is to have at least a couple of crystal balls that have auspicious images, mantras or sutras lasered on to the crystal. Or to display a large crystal ball that has the globe would also be beneficial to sign.

Remember that crystals are a very effective empowering medium and above all things crystals bring harmony and a sense of loving kindness in to the home. So this is something we do recommend strongly.

Displaying **six smooth crystal balls** (around 2 to 3 inches in diameter will do, although it is often good to have one super large crystal ball) in the home always brings harmony and enhances loving energies.

39

In 2012, this is one thing that would be extremely beneficial to bear in mind.

In 2012, it is also a great idea to activate the power of Fire element inside the home as this element, which represents intelligence and creativity, is missing from the feng shui chart. Enhancing the home with strengthened Fire will activate the good star numbers of the chart. You can do this by introducing a **red crystal ball** placed amongst the rest of them on your coffee table. You can also add more light into the heart of your home. Consider installing brighter light bulbs or bringing in white lamp shades that create pockets of lit up area through the spaces of your home.

Also add extra light to the **Southwest** corner of the home. Adding to the brightness of the SW sector strongly enhances the matriarchal energy while subduing the hostile star number 3 which flies there in 2012. This will strengthen the mother energy of the home, which benefits the mother figure of the family, and these benefits extend to the entire family.

THE FLYING STAR CHART OF 2012

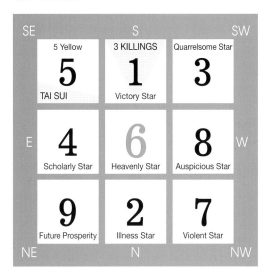

The chart shown here reveals how the nine numbers of the original Lo Shu square are laid out in the different sectors of the home for 2012.

This is probably the best way to understand the feng shui pattern of the year, as it shows how energy congregates within any built-up structure. The nine numbers laid out as shown should be superimposed onto the layout plans of homes and offices in order to understand the luck of sectors, corners and rooms in the home or office.

> Every level of the home is affected by the chart, so it is necessary to superimpose the chart on every floor level of your home/office.

Each of the numbers carries energy which can be auspicious or unlucky. The numbers have an intrinsic meaning which reflects luck patterns congregating in each of the different compass sectors of the home. Feng shui practitioners are familiar with all the afflictive and auspicious natures of the nine numbers; and lineage texts on feng shui offer specific ways of subduing the bad numbers and enhancing the lucky numbers.

This is basically how the feng shui of homes are updated and improved each year. It is a method that has not failed, so each year, the updating procedures to ensure feng shui continues to be good requires the chart of the year to be analyzed and acted upon.

Enhancing the 6 in the Center

The most important thing to do first is to strengthen the center number 6, which is auspicious, and this we have already done by **increasing lights** in the center and displaying **Earth element energy** here with crystal balls or other auspicious images made of crystal.

If you can afford them, you can display crystal images that have genuine 24 carat gold embedded within. This is extremely lucky for the everyone within the household and also attracts wealth and prosperity luck for the family.

Strengthening the 1 in the South

The Victory Star 1 flies to the South, bringing good fortune success luck to bedrooms located here in 2012. So if you sleep in such a room, you will enjoy the luck of victory and success. You can also place the **image of a Horse** here, as the Horse brings the hidden powers of courage and endurance to the South.

Displaying the **Banner of Victory** in the South corner of the living area or having a small water feature here are other excellent ways to cause the power energy in the home to manifest. This will be especially beneficial to the young women of the family - i.e. the daughters of the family.

Activating the 8 in the West

All those whose bedrooms are located in the West sectors of their home will benefit from the powerfully potent number 8 star, which flies into this corner in 2012. Here, the auspicious effect of the 8 star is strongly magnified by the *Yi Duo star* which has also flown here brought by the compass stars of the 24 Mountain directions.

The 8 star also benefits all those whose main entrance door into their homes are located in the West sector of their home. You can then enhance the foyer area of your home with brighter lighting as fire enhances the earth element of the 8 star. You can also place a red **crystal ball with sutra** here or in your West-situated bedroom to activate the power of 8. Also try and keep the door opened as much as possible to let the energy of 8 flow in.

Note that using the Fire element to activate the 8 star also subdues the Metal element of the West. Metal weakens the Earth star 8, so having it subdued will enhance the balance in favor of the 8 star. The advice given here also benefits all those with offices located in the West part of their building.

For those looking for more things to display in the foyer to improve the auspiciousness of their abode can also place the liu li figure 8 here; or an image of the **Phoenix**. This not only activates the West sector but also the presence of the Rooster in the year's paht chee chart.

Good feng shui is very much about enhancing the energy patterns of the home, and placement of the correct symbols in the correct corners of the home does go a very long way towards doing this.

Nurturing the 4 in the East benefits Rabbit

Contrary to what some believe, the number 4 does not bring negative connotations or bad luck under the flying star system of feng shui, and in fact, this is the number most often associated with peach blossom or romance.

Feng shui traditionalists regard this as the number which enhances the chances of marriage within families whose main entrance doors face its location, and for those whose bedrooms are placed where it flies into for the year. In 2012, the number 4 flies to the East.

The element of the East is Wood, which is in harmony with the element of 4, which is also Wood. But the energy of the number 4 star is not strong. This is because it is also affected by the *Star of Reducing Energy* brought by the compass stars of the 24 mountains. As such, it is advisable to strengthen the number 4 star with Water element energy here.

Placing a water feature here is one way of doing this. So if your home is facing East, or if your main door is placed in the East sector of the home, having water element energy here would be very helpful in activating the positive attributes of the 4 star.

A water feature in the East will strengthen the positive aspects of this flying star. Just ensure you do not install a water feature that is too big for your home, as this will overwhelm the home and create an imbalance.

Those born in Rabbit years benefit from their very strong Life Force and inner Chi Essence this year. So for you, the influence of the *Reducing Energy Star* is not so potent and certainly not potent enough to harm you or cause you to lose steam during the year.

Note that the number 4 is also regarded as the *scholarly star*, bringing luck to all kinds of academic pursuits. If your family comprise children or teenagers still at school or in College, nurturing the number 4 star with a small water feature brings them good fortune luck to their studies, in their examinations and to their applications for admissions into reputable Colleges.

It is however worthwhile noting that the water features used must not be too big, otherwise the number 4 can turn ugly, bringing the affliction of infidelity and sexual scandal. So keep the presence of water here properly balanced.

Magnifying the 9 in the Northeast

This number represents "future prosperity". It is also the magnifying and expanding number which expands both good and bad. Note that the intrinsic element of 9 is Fire, another reason it is so welcome here in the Northeast. The Fire element enhances the sector's Earth element, strengthening the energy of this part of the

47

house. If your bedroom is located here, you will enjoy all the benefits that the number 9 brings, including the luck of permanence to all the good luck you successfully build on.

If your door faces Northeast or is located in the Northeast sector of the home, it will be very beneficial to **add lights** to this sector at the start of the year. Enhance the lighting of the doorway area of the home both inside and outside. Doing so will magnify the long term luck prospects of the family.

The Northeast 1 sector benefits very much from extra Fire element that gets created here. So do place extra lights in this corner; better yet, place the Hum lampshade or place something a bright red in color here - perhaps red cushions, curtains or a red dominated art piece.

ENHANCER: Anyone living in this part of any building is sure to benefit from placing **bright lights** here. This will attract powerful yang chi and fire energy which ensures the sector benefits form the number 9 star here.

Subduing the Illness Star 2 in the North

In 2012 the illness star 2 flies to the North, bringing the sickness affliction to all those whose bedrooms are placed in the North of their homes. And if the front door is placed in the North sector, then the effect of this affliction affects everyone living within.

The illness star is an Earth element star, **and happily, its flight into the North does not strengthen it**, unlike last year when the illness star in the South brought a great deal of sickness to many people.

Nevertheless, it is a good idea to subdue this affliction as it is never pleasant getting sick or succumbing to the fever bug, the coughing bug or the flu bug. Worse, the illness star weakens the resistance of all those whose life force or chi energy is not strong.

CURE: Wear the **anti-illness amulet** medallion or the protective amulet specially made to protect against succumbing to physical ailments.

Suppressing the 5 Yellow in the Southeast

Those familiar with feng shui afflictions know how awful the yellow star 5 can be. This is the star number that brings a whole series of bad news, illness, obstacles to success and all kinds of depressing feelings. It creates an aura of despondency and unhappiness, and causes moods and attitudes to just go haywire. It rarely surprises us when those affected by it start being more sensitive than usual to imagined slights, or who become extra prone to finding fault with others.

In 2012 this affliction affect those whose bedrooms or whose main doors into their homes are situated on or facing the Southeast direction. Do be very mindful of this affliction if it affects you.

CURE: A good cure continues to be the **five element pagoda embellished with the Tree of Life** which we introduced last year. This pagoda continues to be a powerful remedy for this afflictive star. In this year of the Dragon however, it is also very beneficial to add the **powerful seed syllables** associated with purifying Fire energy, as this has the added advantage of engaging the spiritually powerful cures associated with these symbols.

These are the syllables *BAM*, *HRIH* and *AH* which are advised in the Tibetan astrological texts for years when the fire element energy is missing. 2012 is just such a year and homes whose Southeast sectors are thus protected will stay safe from this 5 yellow affliction. Use the **Fire Element Totem pendant** for this.

In 2012, the Fire Totem pendant can be used as a suitable cure for those afflicted by the Five Yellow star. Note that the Fire Totem pendant can also be used as an enhancer and an empowering tool, to give power to one's speech.

Suppressing the Star 7 in the Northwest

The 7 star wreaked some real havoc last year, bringing violence, death and suffering to many countries in the Middle East, as well as into households whose central sector were somehow not protected against this afflictive number.

This year the number 7 flies to the Northwest, directly affecting the luck and prospects of the patriarch of households. This usually refers to the man of the family and to the leaders of countries and companies.

It brings danger of robbery and violence to those living in this part of the home; and in the office, if your desk is located here, chances are you could feel the negativity of being betrayed and let down.

 CURE: The best cure for the 7 star in the Northwest for this year 2012 is water energy. The presence of water near **a Blue Elephant and Blue Rhino** would be extremely auspicious and this is because the metal element of the Northwest strengthens the 7 star. Water is needed to weaken the Metal energy.

Subduing the Star 3 in the Southwest

In 2012, the quarrelsome star 3 flies into the location of the matriarch i.e. the Southwest. This suggests that angry mood swings afflict the mother energy of homes affecting the harmony of families and the safety of marriages. Those whose bedrooms are located here will be especially influenced by this star number.

The number 3 star is a Wood element star and it is best dealt with using Fire energy.

This star number attracts the bad luck of having to cope with problems arising from the law. Court cases, litigation and quarrelsome energy will make life extremely difficult and aggravating for you if you are affected by it. If your door faces SW, it is best to try using another door. You should also increase lighting in this part of the house to suppress the number 3 star.

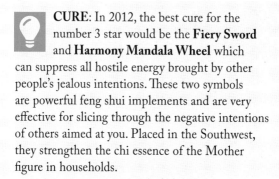 **CURE**: In 2012, the best cure for the number 3 star would be the **Fiery Sword** and **Harmony Mandala Wheel** which can suppress all hostile energy brought by other people's jealous intentions. These two symbols are powerful feng shui implements and are very effective for slicing through the negative intentions of others aimed at you. Placed in the Southwest, they strengthen the chi essence of the Mother figure in households.

24 MOUNTAINS **CHART OF 2012**

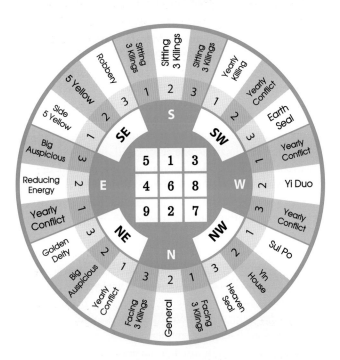

The Stars of the 24 Mountains

We also examine a third set of data which influence what the year brings to each of the twelve animal signs. These are the **compass fortune stars** of the 24 Mountains, which change each year. Their influence on the luck profile of animal signs is meaningful, and working to subdue their negative influences or enhance their positive ones is an excellent way of improving one's fortunes for the year.

Different lucky and unlucky fortune stars fly into each of the 24 compass sectors each year, bringing energies that either improve or decrease the energy of the 12 animal signs.

There are 108 different fortune stars, but only a handful fly into each of the 24 mountain directions in any year. These bring auspicious or harmful influences, which vary in strength and type each year. The stars for 2012 are not as full of promise as they were last year.

This year we see a big number of conflict stars suggesting that the signs affected are in conflict with the year. Conflict signs are not auspicious; nor do they bring anything but disharmony and obstacles, so those affected should strive to either use **amulet or gem**

therapy to counter the potential conflict brought by the compass fortune stars.

Gem therapy uses the power of planetary influences and usually calls on activating one's favorable planets based on each animal sign's lucky days of birth - which can be their *Day of Excellence* or their *Day of Vitality*.

Animal signs that are negatively affected by the stars of the 24 mountains should wear the "gemstone" that activates the planet that strengthens their *Day of Vitality*, and if possible, also their *Day of Excellence*. So it is useful to know the gemstone to wear that will help you subdue 24 mountain star afflictions such as conflict stars, that are stationed at or near your Zodiac sign location.

Each day of the week is ruled by one of the seven powerful planets, which can be activated by wearing the gemstone associated with the planet.

The SUN enhances Sundays and the gemstone which strengthens the energy of the Sun are all the red colored stones - rubies, rubellites and red tourmalines.

The MOON strengthens the energy of Mondays and gemstones associated with the Moon are light colored pearls (preferably white) and the Moonstone. Crystals are also good for nurturing Moon energy to strengthen Mondays.

The planet MARS nurtures the energy of Tuesdays and Mars is associated with red colored stones, although it is coral rather than any of the beryls or crystal stones that strengthens Mars.

The planet MERCURY enhances Wednesdays and gemstones associated with this planet are all the green stones, which include jade, emeralds, as well as green tourmalines.

The planet JUPITER enhances Thursdays and gemstones associated with this planet are all the yellow colored stones, the best of which are yellow diamonds and sapphires, although citrines are also excellent for pacifying Jupiter.

The planet VENUS rules Friday and the gemstones associated with this planet are all the light blue colored stones such as aquamarines and blue topazes.

The planet SATURN rules Saturdays and the gemstones associated with this planet are the dark blue sapphires.

Unfortunately for the Rabbit-born, you are afflicted by the *Star of Reducing Energy* and although you are intrinsically strong this year, nevertheless it is still beneficial and even necessary to enhance your *Days of Vitality and Excellence* as this ensures that your energy synchronizations with the year stay strong. Enhancing your vitality will magnify your luck for the year and keep any conflict energy from harming you.

Wearing faceted **deep blue stones** such as the blue sapphire and **yellow stones** such as the yellow sapphires that catch the light are **most beneficial** for the Rabbit.

Meanwhile also note that your *Day of Obstacles* is **Friday**, so you should refrain from wearing light blue aquamarines or activating the planet Venus, as doing so can bring obstacles into your life.

You can also carry or display the colored gemstones that are lucky for you, and avoid displaying aqua colored blue stones around you.

Watch out for the Three Killings

More serious than conflict stars are the "killing" stars, as these bring killing energy, suggesting serious possibility of loss. In 2012, the stars of three killings bringing three kinds of loss afflict the three mountain sectors of the South. Everyone with doors or bedrooms located in the South should be extra wary and definitely must place the Cure to subdue the *Three Killings* here.

 CURE: The powerful remedy against killing energy are the celestial creatures - **the Chi Lin, the Fu Dog and the Pi Yao.** Images of these three creatures newly made will have fresh and strong energy, and these should be placed in the South corners of the house and frequently used rooms that are located in the South to keep the three killings subdued.

If your staircases and corridors are located in the South, it is a good idea to place the celestials there. Staircases and corridors are conduits of energy. Keeping negative energy out of such areas of the home keeps the household humming along harmoniously.

Other Stars Affecting the Rabbit in 2012

In 2012 the Rabbit sits on the *Reducing Energy Star* and on its right next to the Dragon location is the *Star of Big Auspicious*, which adds a wonderful bonus to you for the year; however on your left next to the Tiger, you have the *Star of Yearly Conflict*.

> In 2012, the Rabbit benefits much from the Dragon who brings lucky energy to you, while the Tiger can be the source of conflict energy sent your way.

The Rabbit can definitely look forward to a year of transformational good fortune following on from the previous year. And on almost every dimension, this is a much better year than last year.

Beneficial Signs

Two other directions benefit from the 24 mountains and these are Southwest 3 and Northwest 3, both of which directions enjoy the good fortune of receiving the **Earth and Heaven Seals** respectively.

The good thing about these seals is that if only just one member or resident of a household enjoys the support of the heaven or earth seal, based on their animal sign - in this case the **Monkey** and the **Boar** respectively - it benefits the whole household.

ENHANCER: It is definitely auspicious to activate the seals and this is easily done by having the Seal of Heaven in the Northwest 3 location and the Earth Seal in the Southwest 3 location. The **Heaven Seal** should be made in Metal and the **Earth Seal** should be made in crystal.

This year's 24 mountains energy pattern manifests only two stars of **Big Auspicious** and these occur in the **East 3** location and **Northeast 2** location. Anyone whose bedrooms are placed in these two lucky directions can expect some big luck this year. For the Rabbit, the NE2 location is your neighbor right next door, so BIG auspicious luck is very near you indeed!!

Always remember that when your personal energy is increased, good fortune gets multiplied more easily and misfortune stars are more effectively subdued. Not many people know that it is **essential to be mentally and physically strong** to benefit from good fortune years. Those whose mental attitudes are stable and strong always attract good fortune a lot more easily than those who give in to frustrations – so try not to get weepy or angry too easily. Some call this intrinsic confidence, and so it is, but confidence comes from having the mental strength and chi essence to stay upbeat and optimistic.

This is why a good store of yang vigor is always needed to actualize good fortune. It is your own confidence and optimism that provides the all-important missing factor, the third dimension to your luck - which is the empowerment of the self.

It is this that makes the difference between having mere mediocre luck, or enjoying truly outstanding luck. Success follows this kind of luck effortlessly.

Keeping Track of Your Good Months

Every year we emphasize the vital importance of timing in the way you manage your year, and in the way you ensure that the important decisions you make as well as the actions you take are made with this in mind through the course of the year. So do remember that the astrological flight of monthly stars is what brings helpful or difficult luck energy.

In these books we examine the way the monthly stars affect each of the 12 signs so that we can include detailed analysis of your luck month by month. This gives you a blueprint for when to lie low and when to strike out, and when to take risks and start projects dear to you.

These monthly analyses also highlight timely warnings that enable you to avoid accidents, avoid meeting up with bad people, getting burgled or succumbing to health risks. Good and bad months for travel are likewise highlighted.

Monthly updates analyze each month's Lo Shu numbers, element, trigram and paht chee luck pillars. These pinpoint your lucky and unlucky months and give valuable pointers on how to navigate safely and successfully through the year. Aggravating obstacles can be avoided; whatever misfortune vibes that lie ahead can be circumnavigated. You can then take timely precautions either by installing remedies or by making sure you wear the necessary protection to avoid these obstacles altogether.

63

The monthly updates are an important component of these books as recommendations are detailed and clear cut. Through the years we have received hundreds of thank you letters from readers telling us how they successfully followed our books and reduced the impact of accidents, burglaries and illnesses.

Improving Luck Using Compass Directions

In 2012, the use of correct facing and sitting directions - i.e. activating your personalized lucky directions - will help you stay protected against inadvertently getting hit by unlucky or disastrous transformational energies. So we have devoted a larger section this year on helping you to get your facing directions right. These are customized to assist all Rabbit-born to finetune their lucky and unlucky Kua directions.

Compass direction feng shui is one of the more effective ways of making sure the energies around you help rather than hinder you, no matter what you may be engaging in through the year. The energies of the 2012 Dragon Year are strong and particularly compelling, with good and bad luck making a big impact on people's lives.

The Dragon's powerful energy needs to be controlled and managed. It is a minefield of a year in terms of belligerence and violence, anger and antagonism; these hostile vibes are strongly prevalent. It is a year when the three celestials - Dragon, Tiger and Phoenix desperately need the calming effect of the celestial cosmic Tortoise. The aura of the Tortoise is legendary and having its presence can be very beneficial. But getting your directions right while sleeping, working, eating, talking and so forth will also go a long way towards safeguarding your luck this year. Do take this advice seriously.

It is really no fun being hit by bad energy; this will happen if you inadvertently face a direction that is out of sync with your sign especially when doing something important or when talking to someone important. The key is to activate directions that are lucky for you and lucky this year as well.

Spiritual Feng Shui

Finally, as something new, we are including in this year's books a whole chapter on powerful cosmic feng shui that suggests a customized amulet that is suitable for the Rabbit sign to wear or display as well as the offering incense ritual to practice.

There are amulets and rituals that ward off bad luck, protect against being obstructed in your business and your career, as well as to attract specific kinds of good fortune for those building a new house, having a baby, starting a new venture, getting married, embarking on a long journey or wanting and needing cosmic assistance on a specific project. Amulets may be worn on special chakra points of the body or displayed in certain corners of frequently used rooms. This is part of the Third Dimension of feng shui, a dimension that makes the practice of feng shui much more complete.

Different animal signs benefit from different kinds of amulets, and wearing those that are best for your sign will help you to stay on top of the elements affecting you during the year.

In astrology, keeping the elements balanced is the key to unlocking good fortune, but when this is helped along by cosmic Sanskrit symbols and powerful mantras, the effect becomes incredibly potent as it taps directly into the cosmic power of spiritual feng shui.

By bringing in the Third Dimension into our luck equation, we will also be enhancing the feng shui of our living spaces. Space is enhanced with environmental feng shui methods through the optimum placement of furniture and auspicious objects.

Good space feng shui also means good design of layout and flow of *chi*. It takes note of compass directions on a personalized basis and uses other methods to identify lucky and unlucky sectors. Broadly speaking, it takes care of the Earth aspect in the trinity of luck.

> The time dimension feng shui address energy pattern changes over time and is founded on the premise that energy is never static but is constantly changing. This means good feng shui requires regular updating by taking into account overlapping cycles of time; annually, monthly, daily, hourly and even in larger time frames that last 20 years and 60 years. It takes 180 years to complete a full nine period cycle of 20 years.

These books address the annual and monthly cycles of change that affect everyone differently. These cycles are viewed within the larger context of the Period of 8 cycle, which deals with the heavenly cosmic forces within the trinity of luck.

Using, wearing and displaying amulets is part of the spiritual third dimension, which focuses on energies generated by mankind. In concert with cosmic forces, the **strength of amulets** is derived from the **individual's own yang chi**, and this is created by the mind's **connections to the cosmos**.

Self energy in its purest form is the most powerful kind of energy. This is **Mankind Chi** which combines with heaven and earth to create the trinity of luck. The empowered self generates copious amounts of positive spiritual chi and this can be directed into amulets to empower them.

When consecrated (i.e. energized) by Masters who possess highly concentrated energies through their superior practices, these amulets take on great potency.

To possess concentrated spiritual power requires years of practice; there are methods - both gross and subtle - that can be learnt which are collectively part of the **inner feng shui** traditions of feng shui.

In the old days, Masters of the old school were great adepts at these kinds of transcendental practice and they often made special amulets with their knowledge, to give to those who came to them for help. Some of these amulets were made according to the animal sign of birth of those asking for them.

These Masters were devotees of Taoist or Buddhist spiritual deities; many increased their own cosmic powers through regular daily meditations, reciting powerful mantras and sutras and using secret rituals to remove obstacles. In the practice of astrological traditions, the **Tibetan practitioners of cosmic magic** generally invoke powerful Buddhist deities who awaken within these individuals their own inner forces, sometimes bringing them to pretty high levels of siddhic accomplishments.

This aspect of feng shui, or luck invocation has only rarely been leaked out into the world. Many of the most effective methods and rituals, sutras and magical mantras are still secret, or have not yet been translated. Masters familiar with these practices reveal their secrets only to a favored few.

But already, many of these "secrets" are fast permeating city life in the great western capitals of the world - New York, London, Paris, San Fransisco and Los Angeles and so forth where shamans - or practitioners of what is being increasingly referred to as soul magic are increasingly being consulted.

We have discovered that the Tibetan way of using powerful meditation techniques accompanied by specific rituals of chanting can bring some excellent results; and particularly good for pacifying troubled energies, increasing abundance energy, controlling fierce wind energies or for subduing harmful energies. We address some of the easier methods of doing so in the last part of the book.

The most important component of these rituals is to develop a respect for the environment around us; and also respect for the eight direction Earth Spirits who can be invoked to keep homes protected and auspicious.

Some of these powerful secrets and ways of incorporating them into daily life to enhance our state of abundance have made their way to us. One discovery we relate to is in creating and consecrating amulets, and filling them with powerful relic pinnacle mantras as well as mantras according to the animal sign of birth.

You can also use incense offering rituals to overcome life and success obstacles. These specially formulated incense contain ingredients which many of you may not be familiar with.

But the "secrets" of offering incense that include details of the natural herbs and precious substances that are burnt as offerings to the different wind and earth spirits are aspects of Tibetan feng shui that are beyond the scope of this book.

What we have put together are compressed incense using formulations to appease local spirits and to clear obstacles that may be blocking your success luck.

For the Rabbit, we recommend you use incense to clear all bad luck afflictions during the months of **February, March, July, September, November** and **December** this year. Doing incense offerings during these months enable you to subdue a variety of negativities including conflicts, illness and burglary aggravations.

71

Special amulet for the Rabbit. Keeping this amulet near
you at all times will protect you from harm and from the
bad intention of others.

Chapter Two

THE RABBIT IN 2012
Luck Prospects &
Energy Strength

- Earth Rabbit – 73 years
- Metal Rabbit – 61 years
- Water Rabbit – 49 years
- Wood Rabbit – 37 years
- Fire Rabbit – 25 years
- Earth Rabbit – 13 years

Outlook for the Rabbit In 2012

All the elements that signify the five types of luck change in 2012, reflecting the transformational nature of the year's energy. For the Rabbit, the new set of energies bring substantially improved luck. Life force and inner chi improves significantly and the Rabbit is certain to recover whatever ground may have been lost last year. Other categories of luck also show improvements.

With life force and chi essence improving so significantly, your luck profile for the new year changes dramatically. Overall luck also improves, and for some of you, financial and success luck perks up quite substantially. Many of you will also enjoy good health this year, so it is a perfectly good time to indulge yourself in physical activities, travel or engage in strenuous-type hobbies.

Meanwhile, the Tiger's continued presence in the Paht chee chart of the year indicates the continuation of the Tiger as a significant force and this benefits the Rabbit because with the Dragon and Tiger in the chart, the Rabbit is able to create the **Seasonality of Spring**. This is very auspicious for the Rabbit and is another indication of great good fortune. Whatever the Rabbit does this year that is initiated in Spring will grow, blossom and take fruit.

This year's most successful Rabbit will be the **37 year old Wood Rabbit** who can look forward to a great year that brings exceptional Finance and Success luck. This coupled with your strong chi essence and life force will give you the stamina and the spirit to "accept" all the goodies coming your way. Another Rabbit having extremely good indications in its element chart is the **13 year old Earth Rabbit** who enjoys very positive improvements in every aspect of your life. For you, this too is a year to look forward to.

For all the other Rabbits, this is a year to be retrospective and to think through situations. The year favors a philosophical and even strategic way of doing things. The Rabbit does however benefit from beneficial feng winds as well as strong inner convictions; these added together enable you to generate a special enthusiasm that lends exciting yang chi to all that you do. As a result, good fortune energies are not difficult to come by.

Feng shui flying stars bring a comfortable homely ambience for you, so the year becomes rather protective and matriarchal - this means there is nurturing energy for those already married and quite excellent marriage luck for the singles. In fact the Rabbit's good fortune showcases quite a spectacular revival over the previous year. Just note that in this Dragon Year, the greater Universe brings transformational energies, so if at times you feel uncertain, it is your inner voice of caution speaking to you... follow your instincts, because your chi essence is at a good level. There is never any harm in being careful and circumspect. This thinking before acting is certain to benefit you.

The luck of the five kinds of Rabbit based on the element interactions of their heavenly stems with that of year indicates as follows. This reflects the Rabbit's overall luck quota for the year:

Metal Rabbit – Good health & happiness
Water Rabbit – Luck and life are stable & exciting
Wood Rabbit – So good you cannot wish for more!
Fire Rabbit – Opportunities turn sour with impatience
Earth Rabbit – Everything is going just swell

OUTLOOK FOR THE RABBIT IN 2012

The Rabbit has good things coming as well as some pretty excellent instincts to see you auspiciously through 2012. Listen to your own inner voice and your own common sense, and do not have light ears taking advice from any and everybody. Most importantly, do not be your own worst enemy, pricking your own bubble and destabilising your own sense of self worth.

You must know well enough that when your personal energies synchronise in a balanced way with the energies of the year, that generally, your judgements for that year will be sound and the actions you take will bring good results. So you can be as aggressive as you wish in pursuing fresh pastures professionally and commercially. Irrespective of where you work and what you do, whether you are a business person or working for someone or for some company, this is a year when your personal elements are bringing you good fortune.

With this kind of outlook life looks quite brilliant indeed and with your higher energy levels, you are also able to go the extra mile. Just always be aware that the greater cosmic energies of the year are bringing along a scenario of change to the year. There are also major afflictive stars that cause even the best laid plans to go awry during the year so if anything happens to force you to change directions, it is wise to accept this and go with the energy flow of the world.

The year 2012 is a powerful transformational year, and it does everybody good to go with this transformational flow rather than attempt to fight against it. If yours is a good year as it is whatever changes come your way will work out well.

In 2012 the Rabbit is influenced by one *Big Auspicious* (in East 3 location) and one *Yearly Conflict* (East 1) Star. So you are actually sandwiched between one excellent and one *Quarrelsome Star*.

So first you need to overcome the *Star of Yearly Conflict*. This is brought by the 24 mountains and is an unfriendly star. This star affecting the Tiger side of you in East 1 location. Be wary of this and know that you must walk away from potential conflict situations despite being provoked. With this star around, whatever misunderstanding or quarrel may develop in your life has the potential of developing into something big.

CURE: You can display any of the three celestial guardians - **the Chi Lin, Fu Dog and Pi Yao** - in the East 1 sector of your home. This will keep the conflict energy subdued. Ensuring protection against afflictions of this kind enables you to take fullest advantage of the "goodies" that come into your life in the new year.

As for the star that is lucky for you, this is the *Big Auspicious Star* which is extremely beneficial especially during a year when you also benefit from the power of string *chi* essence and life force. The presence of this star so near your home locations suggests that something very enticing and with plenty of growth potential is just round the corner, is coming to you. Do be very mindful of this without expending excessive energy on expecting it. Be relaxed in your vigilance at opportunities coming, but also refrain from over anxiety.

FENG SHUI ENHANCER: To benefit from *Big Auspicious Star*, you can consider placing something red in its own East 3 corner as this will create much needed fire energy that is so lacking this year. Display a red crystal ball with Heart Sutra OR place the Hum lampshade here. The all powerful *Hum* syllable, kept activated by the light of the lampshade is very auspicious and it can jumpstart the luck of the star. Keep the lampshade turned on everyday and if you can, add some other **crystal globes** under the lampshade as this will bring great harmony into your life and into your home. Crystal balls have an enormous capacity to absorb conflict vibes, especially when there is a light activating them. This should take care of the *Yearly Conflict Star* on the other side of your home location.

While you place these enhancers, also make the effort to keep all the other lights in your East location of the house or living room a little brighter than usual as this adds to the store of fire element energy.

The Rabbit is definitely enjoying a good year in 2012 both professionally and in your personal life. Those who are married might see a "happiness occasion" i.e. maybe a new baby or a marriage of one of your children. Should there indeed be such a *hei* occasion in your household, welcome it as a very good sign. You can also create such an occasion by throwing a yang evening of festivity celebrating a birthday of an older person.

As for your relationship luck, this too is favorable and you will appear both charming and likeable to others. They respond very well to your greater sensitivity, and also to your more confident aura. Happily for you, 2012 is a year when you have a lightness to your step, and a keen sense of enjoyment. You will also be very sociable this year relating well to many people.

For your own happiness however what the year holds most for you is that you will rise to new challenges with confidence. This means a great deal to you -

to be able to run faster, have greater stamina and achieve tangible results in whatever you do. It enriches your view of yourself and brings you a wonderful sense of well being.

For many of you, this is also a year when love can come knocking. To those not yet committed in a relationship, there can well be romance and the potential of romantic attachments coming your way OR perhaps someone in your social circles declares a love for you that you never suspected OR maybe a chance meeting you did not think could develop into anything serious actually doing so.

This year it benefits you to be quite overt in your ambitions; to go after bigger challenges with larger payouts because it is a good year for you. The Rabbit is most effective and successful when it runs faster and longer than its competitors,

Also note that in 2012, pairing up with your seasonal partners the Dragon and Tiger can be beneficial. This brings you the great advantage of the power of Spring!

OUTLOOK FOR THE LADY RABBIT IN 2012

The Rabbit lady in 2012 is a sharp and very alert individual who can spot new opportunities easily and gear herself to action with verve and vitality. The year's energies are excellent for her. Her judgement is good and her instincts are spot on, so this is potentially an excellent year for her to shine brightly. For those of you in your prime and working professionally, this is a year when there are advancements, promotions and more money coming your way. You will actually be overwhelmed by all the good things coming to you, so that in many ways, your view of the world might

BIRTH YEAR	TYPE OF RABBIT LADY	LO SHU NO.	AGE	LUCK OUTLOOK IN 2012
1939	Earth Rabbit Lady	7	73	Extremely good year. Great abundance.
1951	Metal Rabbit Lady	4	61	Everything moves smoothly.
1963	Water Rabbit Lady	1	49	Great success luck motivates you.
1975	Wood Rabbit Lady	7	37	Superlative year. Finances excellent.
1987	Fire Rabbit Lady	4	25	Success for sure. Unstable finances.
1999	Earth Rabbit Girl	1	13	Productive & satisfying year

become too rose-tinted. Be careful not to get careless or excessively hasty.

Note that the Lady Rabbit is very much a creature of Spring, working best during this time of the year and also when its Spring associates - the Dragon and Tiger - blend in a balanced way with you. In 2012, it is a good idea to be extra watchful and alert during the Spring months, as this is the time that favors you.

In your relationships with others, you will find it easy to be gracious, good mannered and kind, and you will carry yourself with all the elegance that has come to be associated with you. Looking at you, many will know you are in a very good place in 2012 as not only is your personal luck strong but your inner spirit is also soaring high. So your body language will be that of a winner pleased with the world. The signs indicate that your chi will attract all the right people into your life helping you and supporting you.

The female of the Rabbit sign always has a pleasant personality - this year, she benefits more from her relationships than ever before. All her networking skills come together working brilliantly well for her, so from this standpoint, it becomes a hugely satisfying year indeed.

From a financial and success perspective however, it is the **37 year old Wood Rabbit lady** who benefits the most from the year's good energy. This becomes her year to shine, gain top honors and be singled out for recognition, way beyond her own expectations. Indeed, this could well turn out to be quite a transformational year for this Rabbit lady. Achievements and accolades gained this year will last for a long time indeed.

The 25 year old Lady Fire Rabbit has a great year from a Success standpoint. You will achieve all that you set out to do, even if financial luck is not always stable and can even cause you some stress. This could affect your health and wellbeing or it could also work the other way round, that some kind of illness might eat into your finances in a serious way. As such you MUST avoid staying in a North-located room which houses the illness star.

You should also make efforts to take care of your health as this can cause obstacles to an otherwise great year. The good thing is that your life force and inner essence are at high levels, so there is no real danger; and in terms of success luck, you are doing fine. So professionally, this a good year.

The 13 year old teenager Earth Rabbit will enjoy an outstanding year filled with recognition luck. You benefit very much from all the element relationships in your life having good sync energy with the year and you will find that you are very well positioned to take fullest advantage of all that comes your way. Some truly brilliant money and success luck in this year of the Dragon. So perhaps there could well be a scholarship of sorts on the horizon - in any case, this is a year when hard work pays off brilliantly.

The older Rabbit ladies will also find the year to be most satisfying. Those past their sixties need not worry about finances or security as there is plenty of leisure time alongside socialising that brings satisfaction and happiness.

OUTLOOK FOR THE GENTLEMAN RABBIT IN 2012

The Gentleman Rabbit is almost always an agreeable fellow, although he often has a tendency to look distracted, his attention seemingly engaged elsewhere. Rabbit guys are always much better off married or in a serious relationship with someone than being single. They flourish under the care of a matriarchal presence - and they also tend to be very easily influenced by the nurturing mother figures in their lives. But married or not, Rabbit men tend to be dreamy. They are great thinkers but need someone to push them on.

BIRTH YEAR	TYPE OF RABBIT MAN	LO SHU NO.	AGE	LUCK OUTLOOK IN 2012
1939	Earth Rabbit Man	7	73	Satisfying year filled with happiness
1951	Metal Rabbit Man	4	61	Great health & good success luck
1963	Water Rabbit Man	1	49	Very successful achievements this year
1975	Wood Rabbit Man	7	37	A fabulous year! Money & success luck.
1987	Fire Rabbit Man	4	25	Attainments come but no money luck
1999	Earth Rabbit Boy	1	13	A year of recognition & achievements

So in terms of taking the initiative, the Rabbit gentleman in 2012 who has a strong woman behind him will tend to do better than those without this presence.

The Rabbit guy is good at hiding his real feelings. He does not take kindly to criticism. And in fact tends to harbor a natural aversion to those who belittle him in anyway. As a result, he is usually not suited for high political positions. If he takes on too much responsibility he very definitely will wilt under pressure unless those close and dear to him are there to "prop" him up.

Happily in 2012 he benefits very much from a strong Life Force and Chi Essence. The quality of his chi is excellent and this gives him strength and willpower, so that he will surprise even himself, given the new level of confidence surging through him.

Rabbit Gentlemen in the prime of their career will find themselves taking the initiative to advance themselves in whatever they are pursuing. For the **49 year old Water Rabbit guy**, there is plenty of attainment luck and above average monetary gain of some kind. Your business acumen makes this a year of many triumphant moments.

The younger 37 year old Wood Rabbit guy will enjoy even better times. For you, this promises to be a financially outstanding year when money and abundance are at an all-time high. It is the same with your Success luck - this too is scaling the heights, so 2012 could well turn out to be a benchmark year for you.

The 25 year old Fire Rabbit might get married, or at least engaged this year. It is a year when emotional commitment and a strengthened personal life brings much happiness. If still single, it would be auspicious to hook up with that someone special. For those already married, it is an excellent year to have a baby.

All Rabbit guys benefit from their enhanced energy levels. Financially, prospects for making gains are very promising this year. Definitely from an economic viewpoint, things look extremely stable. The year's level of success luck is very much improved over last year and there are happily very few obstacles making life difficult for you. For those in your prime, some sort of recognition will be coming, and for the younger Rabbits, there are excellent developments in your private life bringing lots of happiness.

ENERGY STRENGTH ANALYSES OF RABBIT LUCK 2012

This section focuses on the element luck analyses of the Rabbit in 2012. These reveal five kinds of luck in the Rabbit horoscope and are charted according to how the Rabbit's ruling luck elements in the year of birth interacts with the elements of the year 2012, thus offering indications of strength or weakness in the horoscope for the year.

Check the tables applicable to your type of element Rabbit to take note of the state of your five luck categories in 2012. The significance of the luck indications is explained as follows:

First, Your Life Force...

This highlights hidden dangers that can be the cause of premature death. Danger to one's life can manifest suddenly and unexpectedly, with little warning. In the past two years, clashing elements in the paht chee chart brought raging wild fires, widespread floods, massive earthquakes and other natural disasters wreaking havoc and destruction. Last year, this was compounded by the feng shui chart which brought the *Violent Star 7* to the centre, so we saw raw human anger overflow into revolution that brought danger into the lives of millions of people. Much of these uprisings and disasters happened without warning. Staying safe against being caught unawares is an important aspect of horoscope readings. This is the perspective within which your life force luck must be seen.

For all those **born in Rabbit** years, your Life Force luck shows a very healthy **OO** for 2012 and this means that your life force is very strong, and the year should be reasonably safe for you. You need not have to worry despite the turbulence of the world's energies & the instability of natural forces.

Second, Your Health Luck...

This is the luck of your health condition during the year and it indicates how strongly you can avoid illness bugs. For the Rabbit, note that the feng shui chart brings good strong winds that support rather than cause you illness afflictions.

Only **25 year old Fire Rabbit** needs to be particularly careful as you have a **XX** against your health. All other Rabbits remain pretty strong. When the luck indication is a double cross XX, it means that 2012 can bring ailments and vulnerability to health issues, and these could cause obstacles to work schedules. Plans get blocked and opportunities get missed. Poor health luck means you can get food poisoning easily, and you could catch wind borne diseases. It is advisable that **25 year old Rabbit** use a cure against illness. This is either the **wu lou** or the **vase with healing nectar**.

But for all others and especially for the **61 year old Metal Rabbit**, your health luck is superlative and it promises to be a very energetic year for you indeed. The **49 year old Water Rabbit** has a **OX** showing, but this is not a cause for too much worry, as the **O** always supersedes the **X** for matters pertaining to health. So basically all the other Rabbits should go through the year with few serious health problems.

Third, Your Finance Luck...

This reveals if you will enjoy financial stability during the year. It is also an indication of whether you can do better than the previous year. All indications for the Rabbit this year is that money luck is flowing your way. To start with, all Rabbits will experience a big improvement over the previous year, and for the **37 year old Wood Rabbit**, financial luck is at the maximum level this year. Your star is rising with sources of revenue multiplying quite noticeably and substantially. You show a triple **OOO** and this means that very substantial gains of new wealth is coming to you in 2012.

The other Rabbit having great good fortune in this aspect of their luck is the **13 year old Earth Rabbit** who enjoys the luck of two circles i.e. **OO**. Viewed against the rest of the chart, you also enjoy plenty of all-round luck as well.

A single circle – **O** – means the year does not bring much change to your finances and you will enjoy a stable situation. There are few surprises to make you worry. This will be the case for **50 year old Water Rabbit**. An indication of crosses is a negative reading and the more crosses there are, the greater the instability of your financial situation. Only one Rabbit i.e. the **25 year old Fire Rabbit** has

The White Dzambala moving mantra watch .

this showing. One of the best ways of enhancing wealth luck is to invoke the presence or energy of the Wealth Buddhas, either the **Yellow Dzambhala holding a Rat spewing forth jewels**; or the **White Dzambhala sitting on a Dragon**. Wearing these images - as a watch for instance, with their mantras perpetually moving - is one of the best ways of activating wealth luck. It is an also excellent spiritual feng shui aid for the Dragon Year.

Fourth, Your Success Luck...

This highlights your attainment luck for the year whether it be success in your professional work or in your studies. Circles are strong indications of success, while **XX**s are negative indications suggesting obstacles. The luck indication for all of you born in Rabbit years is that you enjoy a fabulous triple OOO indication and this means you will all enjoy a highly stable year at work. Your professional life moves along smoothly with few distractions or hindrances. As a result, success will not be too difficult to come by and there is also a great deal of positive acknowledgements of your contributions. People become aware of your talents and capabilities. There will thus be upward mobility for quite a number of you. A **OOO** indication is usually considered a very reliable indicator of exceedingly good fortune within the category indicated.

Fifth, Your Spirit Essence...

This indicator of chi essence luck reveals insights into your inner resilience and spiritual strength. When strong, it shows you are resistant to spiritual afflictions and can more easily overcome the lack of other categories of luck. Low Spirit Essence, indicated by crosses, is a negative indication.

The Rabbit however has a double **OO** chi essence so your inner spirit is very strong. This is excellent and you should make it stable by wearing protective seed syllables touching your body. These are best worn as a pendant touching your heart chakra. Seed syllables include the extremely powerful *Hum* seed syllable but also the *Tam* syllable or any one of or all three of the syllables *Om*, *Ah* and *Hum*. What *Om Ah Hum* does is that when it is worn touching the body, especially at the heart chakra, it seals in all your excellent inner chi essence.

Stabilize your strong Chi Essence this year by wearing the protective seed syllable "Hum".

EARTH RABBIT
73 YEARS OLD

TYPE OF LUCK	ELEMENT AT BIRTH	ELEMENT IN 2012	LUCK RATING
LIFE FORCE	WOOD	EARTH	OO
HEALTH LUCK	EARTH	WATER	OO
FINANCE LUCK	EARTH	WATER	OO
SUCCESS LUCK	FIRE	WOOD	OOO
SPIRIT ESSENCE	WATER	FIRE	OO

METAL RABBIT
61 YEARS OLD

TYPE OF LUCK	ELEMENT AT BIRTH	ELEMENT IN 2012	LUCK RATING
LIFE FORCE	WOOD	EARTH	OO
HEALTH LUCK	WOOD	WATER	OOO
FINANCE LUCK	METAL	WATER	OX
SUCCESS LUCK	FIRE	WOOD	OOO
SPIRIT ESSENCE	WATER	FIRE	OO

WATER RABBIT
49 YEARS OLD

TYPE OF LUCK	ELEMENT AT BIRTH	ELEMENT IN 2012	LUCK RATING
LIFE FORCE	WOOD	EARTH	OO
HEALTH LUCK	METAL	WATER	OX
FINANCE LUCK	WATER	WATER	O
SUCCESS LUCK	FIRE	WOOD	OOO
SPIRIT ESSENCE	WATER	FIRE	OO

WOOD RABBIT
37 YEARS OLD

TYPE OF LUCK	ELEMENT AT BIRTH	ELEMENT IN 2012	LUCK RATING
LIFE FORCE	WOOD	EARTH	OO
HEALTH LUCK	WATER	WATER	O
FINANCE LUCK	WOOD	WATER	OOO
SUCCESS LUCK	FIRE	WOOD	OOO
SPIRIT ESSENCE	WATER	FIRE	OO

FIRE RABBIT
25 YEARS OLD

TYPE OF LUCK	ELEMENT AT BIRTH	ELEMENT IN 2012	LUCK RATING
LIFE FORCE	WOOD	EARTH	O
HEALTH LUCK	FIRE	WATER	XX
FINANCE LUCK	FIRE	WATER	XX
SUCCESS LUCK	FIRE	WOOD	OOO
SPIRIT ESSENCE	WATER	FIRE	OO

EARTH RABBIT
13 YEARS OLD

TYPE OF LUCK	ELEMENT AT BIRTH	ELEMENT IN 2012	LUCK RATING
LIFE FORCE	WOOD	EARTH	OO
HEALTH LUCK	EARTH	WATER	OO
FINANCE LUCK	EARTH	WATER	OO
SUCCESS LUCK	FIRE	WOOD	OOO
SPIRIT ESSENCE	WATER	FIRE	OO

Chapter Three

PERSONALIZING YOUR FENG SHUI LUCK IN 2012

Individualized Directions to Protect Your Good Feng Shui

In 2012 the Rabbit's fortune and feng shui benefits from the its much improved life force and inner essence; also from the embracing feng shui winds that bring new found or rei8gnited love and romance. Rabbits in 2012 also benefit from good scholastic luck. The Rabbit benefits from the Wood element of number 4, which by flying into the Rabbit's East location, enhances its Wood energy, bringing more friends and good relationships in 2012.

The Wood element brings hidden good fortune in the year of the Dragon and in fact Rabbits (37 year olds!) that have Wood as their heavenly stem really enjoy excellent luck this year.

The Rabbit has some special ties to the Dragon Year & the relationship between these two signs is astrological. Together with the Tiger, they create the seasonal luck of Spring. This brings Rabbit an excellent head start in good fortune in 2012. The connection with the Dragon serves Rabbit well in 2012 so that facing the direction East or living in a room here brings excellent feng shui luck.

The energy of the Dragon Year is favorable to the Rabbit, who comes out of the previous year stronger and much revitalised. This favorable energy makes 2012 quite a special year. Gone are the obstacles, hurdles and setbacks of last year.

Associating with the Tiger will also bring good fortune in 2012 as the Rabbit forms a *Ho Tu relationship* with the Tiger, and in a Dragon Year, this becomes excellent feng shui! So the year looks very promising indeed for the Rabbit and these indications alone should bring huge confidence into your mindset. There is every reason for you to prosper and move upwards in this Year of the Dragon.

In terms of feng shui luck, what the Rabbit can do immediately is to give the home a thorough spring cleaning, making sure the energy in all your living and work spaces are not left to stagnate. This is equivalent to five minutes of body shaking each morning, something which experts on energy highly recommend to ensure the chi within our bodies are kept moving each day when we wake up.

> Shift your furniture to move your space *chi*. This allows air to flow through the hidden spaces of nooks and corners and when you are done, move your furniture back. Use this exercise to clean hard to reach spaces. This is a powerful re-energising ritual which encourages energy to move, thus creating yang chi and bringing vibrant new energy into your home.

This is especially important for Rabbit, because last year was simply so stressful, so flushing out the energy of the previous year is extremely beneficial. In any case, this shaking and *chi* moving ritual also makes sure your life does not stagnate and makes sure that you will successfully initiate new projects and grow with a steady and sure hand. It may sound simple, but these simple rituals are very effective.

Next, you can customize the feng shui of your space first by activating the **astrological location** of your animal sign and second by using **compass directions feng shui** to maximise your luck for the year.

MAKING THE RABBIT'S EAST 2 LOCATION AUSPICIOUS

The location of the Rabbit is East 2. You must know exactly where this part of your home is; this is your Rabbit location which you must pay special attention to. You must never for whatever reason at all leave this corner dirty, cluttered or worse, filled with rotting materials.

This part of the home must reflect your care and attention and should definitely not be your store room or toilet. Also, try not to do any cooking in this part of the house or room. It is vital to bring correct feng shui inputs to this part of the home, as well as to this East 2 corner of all the rooms frequently used by you. The element of this space is Wood, while the incoming feng shui wind here in 2012 is also Wood, so this is extremely positive, because not only does this bring friendly strengthening energy to the space, but it also means that your relationships luck will get enhanced significantly in 2012. It is useful indeed to activate the **Wood** energy by infusing your East sector with yang energy - sounds, bright lights and activity.

The Wood element energy here in the East 2 sector benefits the Rabbit whose intrinsic element is also Wood, so there is the luck of comradeship and receiving help and support from peers & colleagues. Significantly also, Fire is the element missing from the chart, and since Wood creates Fire energy, the elements bring an indirect benefit as well.

It is definitely beneficial for Rabbits to enhance their Wood element in the East 2 sectors of their homes by keeping these corners well lit. One thing we really want to recommend is to place a **Double Dragon water feature** here to enhance and keep the Wood element staying strong through the year.

One of the best feng shui ways of strengthening the element of Wood is to have Water element around, so anything that creates the sound of water or has moving yang water is auspicious and thus a good idea. But if you place water here in East 2, also place some **live plants** as well.

 **ENHANCER**: Place the **Tree of Life** here in the East 2 sector as this is an excellent enhancer here. The 2012 tree of life also brings wealth and prosperity luck. It is a young tree that is beneficial this year to signify the season of Spring and also to represent new beginnings – both of which are elements that benefit the **Rabbit**.

Place the Tree of Life in the East sector of the home to bring new opportunities for the Rabbit this year.

ENHANCING YOUR PERSONAL KUA NUMBER

The Kua number of those born in the year of the Rabbit is 1, 4 or 7. Each of the three set of numbers for males or females signify each of the three periods in the feng shui cycle of 180 years. The personalised Kua number interacts with the Lo Shu number of the year and your good luck during the year is either enhanced or afflicted by the way the numbers interact. The Lo Shu number of 2012 is the white number 6. The Lo Shu numbers of those born in Rabbit years are shown below:

BIRTH YEAR	ELEMENT RABBIT	AGE	LO SHU NUMBER AT BIRTH
1939	EARTH RABBIT	73	7
1951	METAL RABBIT	61	4
1963	WATER RABBIT	49	1
1975	WOOD RABBIT	37	7
1987	FIRE RABBIT	25	4
1999	EARTH RABBIT	13	1

Rabbit with Birth Lo Shu of 7
(affecting the 37 & 73 year old Rabbit)

The Lo Shu number of this Rabbit has a neutral relationship with the year's Lo Shu number 6, so it indicates a focusing on relationship luck. Both numbers belong to the Metal element but the 6 brings heavenly luck to this Rabbit as the bond of similar elements can be strong.

Being a West group Rabbit, you will benefit from the NE/SW axis in this Period of 8, and since 7 is the number of the West direction and with the West being so well placed to receive enormous benefits this year, you can increase your feng shui luck just by activating the Earth element in the West. This creates and strengthens Metal here, which benefits the Rabbit with Lo Shu of 7.

To do this, display **crystal globes** with auspicious images and symbols either embedded within or lasered with lucky mantras. Crystals also bring harmony luck to the Rabbit, enabling you to sweeten all your relationships.

Rabbit with Birth Lo Shu of 4
(affecting the 61 & 25 year old Rabbit)

The number 4 creates a **sum-of-ten** combination with the number 6, which brings some excellent auspicious luck to this Rabbit in 2012. This is a very lucky indication, which brings wholeness and completion luck indicating that the year's feng shui has the potential to be truly excellent. It suggests that whatever is started is brought to a successful and auspicious conclusion.

The sum-of-ten combination of numbers is a "special" which also has the power to override many negative implications, so it is a lucky combination indeed. This Rabbit also benefits from activating the East corner of the home with a moving water feature and with a pair of elephants, preferably with the nose pointing upwards. These two symbolically strengthens the space thereby greatly improving this Rabbit's Luck.

Rabbit with Birth Lo Shu of 1
(affecting the 49 & 13 year old Rabbit)

The number 1 creates a **Ho Tu combination** with the year's number of 6. This combination brings relationship luck and can sometimes be read as an indication of marriage if it affects someone of marriageable age. It also brings scholastic or academic recognition. The feng shui enhancement for this Rabbit requires the East corner to be enhanced with water, as water here will bring wealth accumulation luck. But try not to overdo this, as having too much water can sometimes prove to be too much of a good thing. For the 13 year old, Water will benefit work at school, but for the 49 year old, too much water could inadvertenetly cause problems within the marriage.

Finetuning Rabbit's Lucky Directions in 2012

The Eight Mansions formula of feng shui divides people into East and West groups, with each group having their own lucky and unlucky directions. To use Eight Mansions, you need to first determine your auspicious directions and then you should make it a point to always face at least one of your good directions while working, negotiating, sleeping, eating or dating.

There are different lucky directions for men and for women, and these are calculated using their lunar year of birth. Just doing this faithfully, using a good compass to determine the directions will bring you instant good feng shui. This is also one of the easiest formulas of feng shui to use and the one where you are least likely to make a mistake.

Study your good and bad luck directions from the charts in this section. Note that the directions are different for each of the Kua numbers and also note that the Kua numbers are different for Male and Female Rabbits.

AUSPICIOUS DIRECTIONS FOR RABBIT WOMEN

All Rabbit women belong to the West group of lucky directions and many of you are going through an auspicious time in the current **Period of 8**. You benefit from living in SW or NE facing houses, especially houses facing SW1. All recently built SW/NE facing houses bring extreme good fortune to the Lady Rabbit. Indeed, the success direction for all Rabbit women is either Southwest or Northeast.

BIRTH YEAR	AGE	ELEMENT/ KUA	HEALTH DIRECTION	SUCCESS DIRECTION	LOVE & FAMILY DIRECTION	PERSONAL GROWTH DIRECTION
1939	73	EARTH/8	NW	SW	W	NE
1951	61	METAL/2	W	NE	NW	SW
1963	49	WATER/5	NW	SW	W	NE
1975	37	WOOD/8	NW	SW	W	NE
1987	25	FIRE/2	W	NE	NW	SW
1999	13	EARTH/5	NW	SW	W	NE

From now until Feb 4th 2024, houses facing Southeast or Northeast bring brilliant good fortune for their residents.

In terms of facing and living directions, Rabbit women benefit if they sit, work, stand and sleep facing any one of the four directions SW, NE, West or NW and they can select the kind of luck they want and then face the direction that brings that luck. But it is also necessary to finetune these auspicious facing directions as they can be "afflicted" by the year's feng shui winds. Thus take note of the following influences affecting your West group directions in 2012.

- ▶ **The SW** is afflicted by the quarrelsome 3 star. It is NOT a good idea to face SW this year, and in fact doing so could get you embroiled in litigation.
- ▶ **The NE** enjoys the *Star of Future Prosperity*, and living here or facing NE is lucky and auspicious. The luck of this direction is long lasting in 2012.
- ▶ **The West** has the incredibly auspicious prosperity star of 8. This is the best direction of the year! Facing West or living here brings abundance!
- ▶ **The Northwest** is afflicted by the *Burglary Star* and is thus best avoided this year.

AUSPICIOUS DIRECTIONS FOR RABBIT MEN

Not all Rabbit men enjoy the same superior luck which their female counterparts enjoy in the current Period of 8, but those belonging to the West group (i.e. born in 1939 or 1975) do. For them, everything that applies to the women also apply to them. All other Rabbit men belong to the East group, so for them, they should generally use East group directions i.e. North, South, East and Southeast. However in 2012, at least 2 of these directions are hurt by feng shui winds and even though they may be auspicious to your, it is better to avoid tapping into their unlucky vibration this year. Hence, take note of the following influences on these directions in 2012:

BIRTH YEAR	AGE	ELEMENT/ KUA	HEALTH DIRECTION	SUCCESS DIRECTION	LOVE & FAMILY DIRECTION	PERSONAL GROWTH DIRECTION
1939	73	EARTH/7	SW	NW	NE	W
1951	61	METAL/4	S	N	E	SE
1963	49	WATER/1	E	SE	S	N
1975	37	WOOD/7	SW	NW	NE	W
1987	25	FIRE/4	S	N	E	SE
1999	13	EARTH/1	E	SE	S	N

► **The North** is afflicted by the illness star; it is not advisable to face North.

► **The South** is lucky and brings victory energy. You can live in the South.

► **The East** brings excellent *Peach Blossom* & *Scholastic Luck*. Can use this direction.

► **The Southeast** is extremely unlucky. Avoid this sector in 2012.

IMPROVING RABBIT'S FENG SHUI LUCK IN 2012

The quickest way to attract good fortune is to tap your personalized lucky directions. As long as you make sure your lucky direction is not afflicted in 2012, tapping your lucky directions will bring you additional luck that will enhance whatever good fortune may be coming your way, and it will also reduce whatever misfortune luck may be lurking in other parts of your chart. If you cannot tap your best direction, you MUST at least avoid facing a direction that is unlucky for you.

Use an accurate compass when taking directions for feng shui purposes.

Attracting Success

Arrange your work desk so you can sit facing your success direction. Doing so brings you advancement, growth and enhanced stature in your professional life. Just make sure your success direction is not afflicted. For the Rabbit women, note that the West direction enjoys excellent energy, followed by the Northeast direction. These two directions bring success from feng shui winds but the Southwest is hampered by the hostile star 3, which brings obstacles associated with misunderstandings and litigations.

Rabbit Men take note that the Northwest direction is also afflicted in 2012. Here the star of betrayal, burglary and violence is strong, so it is better to avoid it. Sit facing West even if this is not your success direction and it should bring you winning luck in 2012. For Rabbit men whose best direction for advancement is the North, you definitely should not use it in 2012 as this is an afflicted direction. Instead, tap into the victory luck of the South direction as this is the direction that brings success in all your endeavors.

So taking note of the directions that are best for you, you can arrange your desk to face the direction of your choice. But next you must also take note of the arrangements to avoid; always looking out for what is behind you.

You must make sure never to get hurt by something behind you while focusing on facing your lucky directions. In other words watch your back! So...

► Avoid having a window behind you especially if your office or home work area is located several levels up a multi level building. If this is a room on the ground level in your home it is fine.

► Avoid having the door into your room being placed behind you. It is worse if this is your office at work as talk that is detrimental to you get plotted and planned behind your back. This is a severe taboo. For the Rabbit man belonging to the East group, do make sure the door into your office is not facing the Southeast - this would be very unlucky indeed as this is the five yellow direction of this year.

For the Rabbit women and men belonging to the West group, make sure the door coming into your office is not facing NW or SW even if these two directions are lucky for you. Both these directions are afflicted this year, so using these doors can cause obstacles to manifest...

113

▶ Avoid being directly in the line of fire of sharp edges or tables, corners and protruding corners. And definitely DO NOT place your desk at funny angles just to tap into your lucky direction. This can backfire, bringing misfortune luck instead.

Never sit with your back directly facing a door into the room.

Ensuring Good Health

An excellent way to ensure good health in 2012 is to capture your individual good health direction. The secret of good health luck is to sleep with the head pointed to your health direction OR at least one of the four auspicious directions. You should however ensure that your health direction does not suffer from any affliction in 2012.

In this respect, Rabbit women should note that the two West group directions that are hurt by the feng shui winds of 2012 are the Southwest and the Northwest. These two powerful directions are hurt by hostile energies.

So even if these may be your personal health (or other good luck) direction, it is advisable to avoid facing them in 2012. The West and Northwest are fine and are in fact auspicious, because they enjoy the powerful 8 and 9 stars respectively, both of which are good for your health luck.

As for the Rabbit men belonging to the East group, note that only the North is seriously afflicted, being occupied by the illness star, so on no accounts should you face North. Likewise, the Southeast is also seriously hurt by the *Five Yellow*, which also manifests illness of the most severe kind. This too is a direction to be avoided. Remember that sleeping right is one of the easiest of feng shui ways to ensure good health.

The Medicine Buddha watch is an excellent antidote to health woes when the illness star makes an appearance in your chart.

This, plus making certain you are not afflicted by the annual and monthly illness star numbers, is what helps ensure you do not succumb to serious illness.

For all Rabbits, note that the months of **March** and **December** are when you must take good care of your health as these are the two months when you are the most vulnerable.

In those two months, do wear the gold wu lou as this is an excellent amulet against getting sick. You can also wear the Medicine Buddha bracelet which was made precisely to guard against falling ill to epidemics or viruses.

In the Bedroom

To enjoy good feng shui, always be sensitive to the way your bed is oriented and positioned in the bedroom. A golden rule is that beds should always be positioned against a solid wall, and should not share a wall with a toilet or bathroom on the other side. This gives you the solid support you need and the headboard forms a symbolic protective aura that guards you while you sleep. So it is always preferable to have a headboard.

You should make sure never to have toilets on the other side of the wall where your bed is placed. The toilet symbolically flushes away all bad luck and to have it directly behind you while you sleep suggests that all your good luck gets flushed away as well.

Beds that are placed against a wall with space around it are always more auspicious than beds that are wedged tight into corners. Do make sure there are no heavy beams above you as you sleep and no sharp columns hitting at you from protruding corners and cupboards. These cause illness.

And do take note of window views. If you can see blue skies at nights and there is a clear view it is both healthy and auspicious - so also are views of vibrantly growing trees although these should never be too near to your window. But do make sure not to be looking at a dead tree stump or a hostile looking tree outside as these can bring illness into the bedroom.

Becoming a Star at School

For the 13 year old Rabbit teenager, 2012 brings very good success luck and also excellent all-round energy, so the potential for you to emerge as a star certainly manifests for you in 2012. What you need to do to harness extra good luck your way is to make sure you sit facing your Personal Growth direction when you are studying at home, working on an assignment, doing your home work or sitting for an examination. Just make sure you are not facing an afflicted direction!

For the girl, your best direction is Southwest, but in 2012, the Southwest is unlucky, so it is better to face West. Whatever you do, make sure that you always face West in 2012 when tackling any important tasks or when doing homework.

For the young male Rabbits of the East group, your Personal Growth direction is Southeast (**25 year old Fire Rabbit**) or North (**13 year old Earth Rabbit**). Neither of these are very lucky, so it is better to face South to emerge a winner in 2012.

Attracting Romance into your Life

If you are looking for love, there is good news this year in that the *Peach Blossom Star* lands in the East in 2012. This is a powerful love direction for activating marriage luck this year. So no matter your age, irrespective of whether you have been married before, this is an excellent year to set the energy moving to bring you good marriage luck. Those wanting to use this direction to jumpstart their romance luck can place a **bejeweled Rabbit** in their East direction! This is excellent for East group Rabbit men. But if you prefer, you can also tap the South direction. Have your head pointing South this year and place a **bejeweled Horse** on your headboard or behind your bed as you sleep. This should attract love and romance in to your life.

But you can also enhance the energy of marriage luck by using your personalized love direction. For Rabbit women, the love direction is either West or NW… and in 2012, the West direction is very strong while the NW is afflicted, so the advice here is to face the West direction and activate this location with the image of a **bejeweled Rooster**!

For the West group man, your love direction is NE which is also a good direction in 2012, but it is not a peach blossom direction this year, hence you are better off activating the West this year.

The 17 year old Ox teenager can tap into their personal development direction and this benefits their scholastic work because for you, your *Fu Wei* direction is East, which brings excellent study and scholastic luck.

Whatever direction you face, scholastic luck usually comes to those whose sleeping direction are not afflicted by wrong placements - so it is really important to observe sleeping taboos, and always sit facing a direction that is not afflicted in any given year. You also need to avoid facing a direction that causes you to get hit by secret poison arrows.

Ox people belonging to the West group who have the Northwest as their personalized growth direction meanwhile should note that unfortunately for you, this is an afflicted direction in 2012 with the 7 burglary star here. This affliction brings violence, betrayal and robbery and is thus a direction best avoided.

For women, the number 7 also means heartbreak and betrayal so it is advisable to tap another less problematic direction. Another of your West group directions should work better - either West or Northeast. But make certain not to tap into the Northeast direction, as this could cause your life to be mentally stressful. You will find yourself worrying for no real reason at all.

Attracting Romance

Those looking for romance this year can sleep with their heads pointed to their *nien yen* direction. You should also activate peach blossom luck bringing new friends into your life. The nien yen direction also increases your popularity. In 2012 however, if you are a girl, you can tap the auspicious West direction and for guys, you can tap the East direction. Empower these directions with a **Rooster** in the West and a **Rabbit** in the East as these two are *Peach Blossom Animals* that can attract romance luck for you. They are also very strong in 2012!

Rabbit and Rooster images can be used to enhance love and marriage luck this year.

121

Chapter Four

RELATIONSHIP LUCK FOR 2012

Lethargy & stress cause some tension but allies bring respite

How we treat and respond to those we love - our family, lovers, spouse or our children and to those we work with - colleagues, employees, bosses and business associates - depends very much on our relationship energy interacting with others during the year. As such, each year we react to the people around us differently and depending on the influences on our sign the Rabbit, we can be more accommodating in one year and less so in another. This influences our tolerance level and our patience.

COMPATIBILITY
WITH EACH ANIMAL SIGN

COMPATIBILITY	LUCK OUTLOOK IN 2012
RABBIT with RAT	Staying true & faithful despite distractions.
RABBIT with OX	Excellent luck potential for this pair. Ho Tu combination.
RABBIT with TIGER	Synergy luck generate warm loving feelings.
RABBIT with RABBIT	Two of a kind generate warm feelings.
RABBIT with DRAGON	Environmentally-friendly couple stick together.
RABBIT with SNAKE	Hostile sparks fly creating some problems.
RABBIT with HORSE	Too much loving here so need to cool things.
RABBIT with SHEEP	Competitive feelings cause jealousy to emerge.
RABBIT with MONKEY	Not good for each other.
RABBIT with ROOSTER	Surprisingly cordial in a great year for this pair.
RABBIT with DOG	There is mistrust between this pair.
RABBIT with BOAR	Enhancing each other's performance.

Some years we can be very loving and forgiving e.g. like this coming year of the Dragon, feeling at ease with ourselves and with the world, and during other years (for instance last year) we can be less tolerant and also easily stressed out and impatient.

For the Rabbit sign, the year appears is very blessed indeed in respect of most of our relationships and whatever conflict energy may be present to cause distress in interactions with others is completely indirect i.e. caused by unfortunate brushes with others having a harder time of it.

> Feng shui winds do not cause the Rabbit to be anything but accommodating this coming year and the presence of the LOVE star in the Flying Star chart, as well as super strong chi essence, bring a very special kind of relaxing attitude and compassionate influence to all the Rabbit sign's interfaces with friends, colleagues and family.

The Rabbit has a great deal of patience in 2012; as well as enjoying good energy levels, there is also an overriding attitude of goodwill towards others and any kind of direct confrontations is skillfully and smoothly averted. The Rabbit will be very popular in 2012 and much sought after for the positive vibes you exude.

The Rabbit personality is generally calm and diplomatic, although in bad years the Rabbit can be weepy. But in a strong year such as 2012, they are confident and following upon that less sensitive and very accommodating of others.

> In 2012, the Rabbit has a store of tolerance towards everyone, even to the Rooster, its natural astrological enemy. There is a store of goodwill which attracts popularity, so socially the Rabbit is in for a busy year. Happiness in your social life brings a special kind of warmth and younger Rabbits find they are in demand this year. People will gravitate towards you!

The Rabbit will also be on the charm offensive; happily lapping up all the feel-good vibes that surround you and thus cozying up to friends both new and old. Old friends feature strongly in your social life as Rabbits tend to be comfortable with familiar faces; but new friends bring new perspectives so new pursuits and activities open to you. This thus looks to be a very satisfying year for the Rabbit in terms of socializing and partying!

Older Rabbits and younger Rabbits alike are in their element socializing and showing up at parties. The Rabbit sign is at its best when it is networking and making good contacts; single Rabbits will have an extremely happy time checking out all the eligible young people coming their way. Chances of finding romance for the unattached is really very high this year.

This does not mean that there is necessarily marriage chi in the air, but in terms of finding your soulmate, this is a great year for doing so. In the event of there being some kind of romantic union - such as an engagement or a marriage - this year is especially auspicious and it is a good time to bring this kind of great yang chi into your life. It becomes extra meaningful.

Animal signs generally interact in a positive way toward their Zodiac allies, secret friends and astrological soulmates. But the extent of affinity does magnify or get reduced according to the feng shui energy of each sign in different years. So while it is absolutely important to know about these groupings, it is equally important to fine-tune the level of affinity enjoyed each year.

Every sign also has another sign with whom it may be difficult to feel much warmth towards - we call the energy

Arrows Of Antagonism

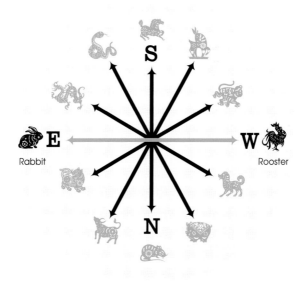

This diagram shows the **arrows of antagonism** within the astrology wheel. It is possible for two animal signs who are "astrological enemies" to get along, when both are going through good years, or when you both have strong inner chi essence in your annual chart.

that flow between them **arrows of antagonism**. It can be troublesome when someone you care for or have just met and feel attracted to belongs to an animal sign that is supposedly your astrological "enemy" - these are signs placed directly opposite you in the Astrology Wheel.

But like it or not, these "arrows" do indeed indicate long term incompatibility unless you can see that animal in other pillars of your Paht Chee! The good news however is that astrological antipathy can get reduced when both signs enjoy good fortune years. Or when both have strong inner chi in their five elements chart. Having said this, it is always preferred for siblings to be astrological allies, so planning your family according to astrological guidelines does create benefits.

Auspicious Crosses

But there is also an astrological "secret" associated with "enemy signs" and this gives families the key to unlocking strong lucky vibes for the entire family. This requires the presence of what is generally referred to as the *Auspicious Crosses* formed by four members within a family unit. These crosses exist in a family when there are two specific pairs of antagonistic siblings or if as in the case of the Rabbit, you can create a very auspicious and major Cardinal Cross should you also have a Rooster in your family.

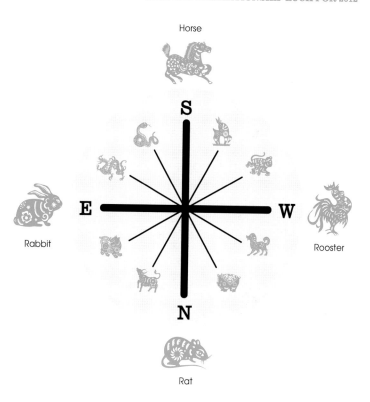

Horse

S

E

W

Rabbit

Rooster

N

Rat

If you have the **Cardinal Cross** within your immediate family unit, this brings an especially auspicious vortex of luck to the family. But all of the four animals that form this cross *must* live in the same house.

Here your antagonistic arrow of antagonism with your Rooster (spouse perhaps?) will be transformed into a luck-generating alliance if you can also have children born in the years of the **Rat** and **Horse**, thereby making up this auspicious cross within your immediate family. This brings together then the four elements of **Wood, Metal, Fire** and **Water** into the family and it is very auspicious.

The Cardinal Cross

For instance for your family, if you are the father or the mother in the family and as you are the Rabbit, your family unit can create the auspicious 4 Element Cardinal Cross which comprises **a Rooster, a Rat, a Horse** and **the Rabbit** (you!).

This requires that you are married to one of these four animal signs and then if you have two children belonging to the other two signs, you would have created within your family the very powerful **4 Element Cardinal Cross**. So, if in your family you already have the first three signs between you, and there is no end of squabbling between your opposing astrological signs, you can try for baby in the relevant year indicating the animal sign needed.

For instance, the next time we see an animal sign that is part of the Cardinal Cross will be in the year of the Horse, which occurs in 2014. By adding a Horse baby

130

to your family everyone gets very fortunate with the potential of the powerful 4 Element Cardinal Cross should there already be a Rabbit/Rooster/Rat in the family. Here we are referring only to the basic family unit and it is necessary for all four signs to live in the same house for the good vibes associated with this Cross to materialize great good fortune.

The Rabbit's Allies

Your allies are the **Sheep** and the **Boar**. In 2012, you will be blessed with powerful high energy which enhances your charisma and your aura. This makes others attracted to you and also makes you the shining star in your trinity of allies. So especially with your allies and your secret friend, the **Dog**, you will be the focal point in 2012.

It benefits your allies to stick closely to you simply because you are of the Rabbit sign exuding strong chi essence. This is a year when the Rabbit is strong and creative, and also very positive, mainly enhanced by good element indications and by excellent feng shui winds as well. The Rabbit also has a special Springtime connection with the Dragon, so you are certain to benefit from the cosmic growth forces of the year.

131

The Rabbit's luck is very forward looking this year, so you should quite easily welcome every new friendship and approach every relationship, new or old, in your life with great eagerness and confidence. Your allies both have mixed luck in 2012 with the Sheep sign having the serious affliction of the quarrelsome number 3 star. This will explain the Sheep's mood swings and hostile nature and you should try to bear with it. Unfortunately, your other ally the Boar is also afflicted by the violent *Robbery Star* number 7 which can bring severe and traumatic loss in 2012. The Rabbit is the hero of the trinity and it is likely that your allies will lean on you for support and assistance. Be understanding!

Your trinity of allies is thus actually quite dependent on you in 2012, as you are the one with the greatest strength; so the Rabbit plays a big role in the trinity. In terms of compatibility, you should make an effort to get along really well with each of your astrological allies, as this lends them strength, resulting in better trust and greater friendship with one another.

To harness maximum benefit from your affinity allies, it is beneficial to carry the symbolic image of your allies. In 2012 the best for the Rabbit born is to carry the image of all three signs together i.e. the Rabbit, Sheep and Boar.

Carry Your Allies Crest Wallet

What will be great is for you to wear or display your allies/secret friend Crest which we have specially designed to place close to you to remind you of their significance in strengthening your energies during the year. The great significance of activating your astrological grouping is often overlooked by many people, so do use the Crest Wallet or brooch not just to remind you but also to activate the essence of the trinity. For the Rabbit, what you need is the Crest of the **Rabbit/Boar/Sheep**.

The Rabbit, Boar & Sheep form an affinity triangle and relationships between you are smooth and productive. Carrying your Crest Wallet enhances this trinity bringing you strong friendship and ally luck.

The Rabbit and both its allies are known for their **gentle diplomacy** and their stoic handling of life's issues. These are the diplomats of the Zodiac who are able to absorb whatever shocks come their way with a philosophical turn of the head. This is a group of animal signs who are fussy and fastidious; you are homemakers par excellent and you possess great moral courage.

Together, the three of you can achieve much. Although you each have your own outer and inner strengths, it is the Sheep who has the most staying power and the Boar who possesses an admirable joy de vivre that is infectious. The Rabbit personality is more ambitious than the Boar, but less ingenious than the Sheep.

AFFINITY
TRIANGLE
OF DIPLOMATS

The Rabbit's allies are the Sheep and Boar, so people born under these signs will generally always be good for you.

The Rabbit, Boar and Sheep tend to be silently confident and very calm personalities. They come across soft and yielding, but they have an inner core of steel and once they make up their minds. As a group, it is almost impossible to shake down any decision they make.

This is a group of people who look out for each other. They may not appear as loyal as the other grouping led by the Tiger, but they are effective and selective in the way they extend out a helping hand to one another.

They are not as competitive as some of the other signs and they are also quite easy going and not at all difficult to handle. As a result, many people like having this trinity of signs working in committees or within specific teams in a work environment.

RABBIT WITH RABBIT
In 2012, two of a kind generate warm feelings

In 2012, two Rabbits are able to create a loving relationship and play happy families with their own kind. These gentle representatives of the Zodiac have a great feel-good attitude this year that is reflected in their sensitivity and care towards each other.

They thus tend to be polite and well-mannered, with each other demonstrating a diplomatic respect which both appreciates; although this kind of proper behaviour might appear to lack warmth, nevertheless the Rabbit sign enjoy this. It is their way of communicating loving energy.

In any case there is instinctive understanding between two Rabbits which establishes a strong base for a solid relationship to grow. Over the years a double Rabbit pairing is likely to strengthen rather than weaken. So they live and work on the same wavelength and between them is unlikely to arise hostility or misunderstandings.

The good thing about the Rabbit personality is that they are rarely hostile creatures. To them, the peaceful approach is always preferred, so in this household there will rarely be any cause for voices to be raised in anger. Should feelings get hurt or anger arise, this is expressed with studied cool. They do not sulk; they merely adopt an air of super indifference. As a result, little is said and this makes it easier to get back together again when anger dissipates.

In this Year of the Dragon, the Rabbit sign enjoys a very smooth ride through the year. Young Rabbits setting out on career paths and not yet veterans of the working world find themselves distracted by thoughts of love and romance. It is that kind of year!

Rabbits are influenced by the *Peach Blossom Star* and with luck on their side, romance and relationship luck make them focus towards their love interests.

Older Rabbits might need to watch out for third party intrusion into their idyll, but Rabbits are strong and confident this year and are thus unlikely to let small misdemeanours get in their way or upset them.

RABBIT WITH SHEEP

In 2012 competitive feelings cause jealousy to emerge

There is no doubt that these two are allies who easily see each other as kindred spirits. But in 2012, there is a great difference in the attitude of these two signs. The Rabbit is relaxed and confident while the Sheep is stressed out and hostile. It is not surprising that resentment of some kind and at some level will creep in to mess up this fine relationship.

> You need to hang in there with each other! This is a pairing where ordinarily you will be waxing lyrical about each other and also enthusiastically digging in to all the fine things that life brings your way.

Ordinarily you would enjoy the good things of life together finding beauty and value in the skies and the mountains. You both like exactly the same things, and you even enjoy going to museums, attending auctions, going shopping, finding gems in flea markets.

This pair of allies will normally get their highs discovering restaurants and fun places, so they are able to create their own world where love flows freely between them. They get bored at the same kinds of things and are stimulated by similar experiences. So here we see an emotional and artistic affinity flowering into deep and abiding love.

But in this year of the Dragon, things do not appear so hunky dory at all. There is hidden resentment and even touches of envy and jealousy - which can cause both parties to get tired and exhausted of one another.

Eventually however, if they can survive a year of noisy quarrels and misunderstandings, this couple is certain to become soulmates capable of bringing great happiness to each other.

To the Rabbit & Sheep, the environment is secondary and work can never take precedence over their concern for each other's happiness. They are genuine allies looking out for each other and easily creating rapport and comradeship. But tempers flare easily and anger simmers beneath the surface over seemingly unimportant things as hostile energies of the year take their toll on you.

It is advisable to each do your own thing this year, and the less said between each other, the better. The Sheep's life is made difficult by the hostile star 3. There is also the yearly killing and yearly conflict stars brought by the 24 Mountains compass, so this is not an easy year for Sheep.

The good thing is that the Rabbit is meanwhile riding along, with none of the stresses afflicting its ally, hence better for this pair to take things easy and let the relationship survive through the year.

 FENG SHUI ADVICE:
The Rabbit might want to consider **wearing red** and **placing the Magic Diagram Red Sword Mirror in the Southwest** to help Sheep subdue the hostility star.

Rabbits in a relationship with a Sheep person can display the Magic Diagram Red Sword Mirror to subdue the quarrelsome energies in the relationship this year.

RABBIT WITH BOAR

In 2012 enhancing each other's performance

The Boar is the other astrological ally of the Rabbit and although there are also afflictions influencing the Boar's behaviour just like with the Sheep sign, nevertheless, 2012 is actually a happier year for the Rabbit involved in a relationship with the Boar. Here, the *Heavenly Seal Star* of the 24 mountains compass brings a calming influence onto this couple.

In 2012 this is a very happy couple between two people who enhance one another's strengths, so benefiting each other for the better. This pair is well suited and the enthusiastic approach to life they both have augurs well for them. This couple is inspiring to watch and their good intentions become very infectious. Others around them respond with similar spontaneous smiles.

It is all very lovely indeed as they generate happiness energy felt by all those around them. They are soulmates loving the same things and motivated by the same kind of people, situations and attainments. Their aspirations are similar, and as a couple it is easy for them

141

to plan outings and holidays. If they get into a work relationship with each other, they will also amalgamate their thoughts and efforts quite efficiently. Outsiders will find it difficult to split them up or cause friction to arise between them.

This is because the Rabbit and the Boar make up two thirds of the trinity of allies described as the Diplomats of the Zodiac. Their calm nature and quiet elegance make them extremely attractive, so they have a good and easy relationship that blossoms in 2012.

What is heart warming for them is their easy communication and also their genuine appreciation of each other's efforts. This couple are "touchy" and "feely"; they love bear hugs, they are demonstrative and they will be explosive in the way they embrace the year's energies.

 FENG SHUI ADVICE: The Rabbit sign enjoys the Peach Blossom Luck this year. To activate this feng shui wind, place the **Double Happiness sign** in your bedroom. If you are in a relationship with someone born in the Boar year, place the **image of the Boar** in your home sign of East. Will do wonders for your relationship with the Boar!

The Rabbit's Secret Friend & Zodiac Housemate

In addition to astrological allies, the Rabbit also has a *Secret Friend* and *Zodiac Housemate* with whom it creates an incredibly special relationship; one that is even more influential than its relationship with its astrological allies. Sometimes your secret friend and Zodiac housemate are the same sign, but in the case of the Rabbit sign, your secret friend is the Dog and your Zodiac Housemate is the **Tiger.**

As a result, the **Rabbit** and the **Dog** have the potential to forge an extremely close and very compatible relationship. They have a lot of time for one another and there will flow between them quite an exceptional sense of comradeship that generates happiness vibes. Even when they are at odds and disagree they are still able to stay close. Secret friends nurture one another, bringing out each other's strengths and potential. It is always beneficial to enter in any kind of relationship with one's secret friend.

As for one's Zodiac's housemate, this generates a pairing with each other that causes the outflowing of hidden strengths and skills. If they are partners in love, or in business, or they are teammates, they create a powerful alliance which brings profits and benefits.

143

The Rabbit's Zodiac housemate is the Tiger, and in this coupling, the Tiger becomes the one who wields the brute strength while the Rabbit uses diplomacy. So together they make a great team. One enforces while one plays the good guy.

What is good about this relationship is that you will find it easy to stick together through thick and thin despite whatever difficulties might confront the both of you. You also bring very good luck to each other.

The Rabbit and Tiger make up the House of Growth & Development, and together they can achieve great things!

144

THE 6 DIFFERENT ZODIAC
HOUSE PAIRINGS

ANIMALS	YIN/YANG	ZODIAC HOUSE	SKILLS UNLEASHED
RAT	YANG	HOUSE OF CREATIVITY & CLEVERNESS	The Rat initiates
OX	YIN		The Ox completes
TIGER	YANG	HOUSE OF GROWTH & DEVELOPMENT	The Tiger employs force
RABBIT	YIN		The Rabbit uses diplomacy
DRAGON	YANG	HOUSE OF MAGIC & SPIRITUALITY	The Dragon creates magic
SNAKE	YIN		The Snake creates mystery
HORSE	YANG	HOUSE OF PASSION & SEXUALITY	The Horse embodies male energy
SHEEP	YIN		The Sheep is the female energy
MONKEY	YANG	HOUSE OF CAREER & COMMERCE	The Monkey creates strategy
ROOSTER	YIN		The Rooster gets things moving
DOG	YANG	HOUSE OF DOMESTICITY	The Dog works to provide
BOAR	YIN		The Boar enjoys what is created

RABBIT WITH DOG
In 2012 mistrust between this pair

These two signs have incredible potential to love each other so much they will indulge themselves silly. In 2012 however, although they are able to enjoy some good times together and even embark on some extraordinary journey in search of spiritual satisfaction, nevertheless, this is also the year when the Dog gets hit with a big zap of distrusting energy, causing life to get complicated.

The number 7 star & the side conflict with the five yellow as well as the direct hit with the **Grand Duke Jupiter** makes the Dog sign extremely suspicious of everyone, including even its own shadow. As a result, relationships of the Dog suffer even with its special friends, which includes you the Rabbit.

This pairing is actually a coming together of "secret friends" so it is generally regarded as a very good and auspicious combination. Marriage between these two signs almost always works well as they are able to see eye-to-eye, agreeing on most things and being very simpatico with one another. It is easy for them to build a strong and stable relationship ,and even if they should separate permanently, this is a couple who will usually stay good friends. But in the Year of the Dragon, the Dog becomes its own worst enemy and Rabbit could well tire of the complications that arise between this pair. Where ordinarily they can rely on each other whether times are good or bad, this year, it seems the hostile winds of the Dragon Year pokes holes in their relationship and goodwill flies out the window!

Their feelings and attitudes cause all kinds of obstacles to come between them. And attempts to split them up or introduce suspicions between them is likely to be successful. The strong Rabbit could walk away and not be able to pull the Dog out of its depression or misery.

The Dog does not have a strong attitude in 2012, as he/she is beset by doom and gloom. The confidence level of the Dog is at a low ebb and what it needs is an understanding shoulder. Within reason, the Rabbit is the best sign to offer this shoulder, but alas the Rabbit is easily distracted away this year...

 FENG SHUI TIP: The Rabbit might wish to take note that the Dog benefits from being protected from the number 7 star so getting a **Rhino or Elephant hanging** will ensure that the Dog feels less hostile or suspicious towards you.

RABBIT WITH TIGER
In 2012 synergy luck generates warm feelings

When Rabbit meets anyone born in the sign of the Tiger, all kinds of positive thoughts immediately flood into the Rabbit's mind. There is hidden connectivity between this pair because they instantly experience a feel-good factor welling up from within them. This feeling is felt more acutely by some and less so by others, but it is felt nonetheless. This feeling reflects their inner intuitive connection, a hidden vibration which acts like a catalyst, bringing out all kinds of warm feelings, skills and goodness which are not immediately obvious.

> Sometimes the pairing between a Rabbit and Tiger is so positive that there is a feeling of instant protectiveness on the part of the Tiger and a simultaneous feeling of safety and security in the Rabbit.

At a surface level, these two signs really make unlikely friends and even less likely lovers or business partners, and this is because the Tiger personality is superficially perceived to be spoilt, loud and demanding, while that of the Rabbit is seen to be docile and gentle; when in truth the Tiger is more of a pussycat and the Rabbit can have the ferocity of a big cat!

148

(*"Soulmate" Potential* ★★★★★)

Superficially, perhaps during the initial stages of their meeting, Tiger's brashness appears louder in the presence of the more quiet spoken Rabbit, but it does not take long for this pair to connect. And this is because the Tiger and the Rabbit are actually Zodiac housemates, who are able to work very comfortably together and in live harmoniously in the same house!

The Tiger and Rabbit have something strong and significant in common. They can even be soulmates. Scratch under the skin of the Tiger to discover a completely deep and complex personality, someone with a vision to build, to create and to develop ideas meaningfully.

This finds resonance with the Rabbit's secret ambition of wanting to do something meaningful with his/her skills; so these two signs enjoy one of best kinds of bonding between two people. They have the potential to be long lasting as a couple.

As a partnership, they complement each other although their modus operandi are different; the Tiger always playing the aggressive role and the Rabbit usually playing the soft spoken compliant soul. But they can easily transform their individual natures into a cohesive and strong partnership.

In 2012 this pair is on a roll. The Tiger is strong but the Rabbit is stronger still, and neither will succumb to jealousy, negativity or insecurity. Both Tiger and Rabbit enjoy powerful inner auras in 2012 because their life force and spiritual essence are well balanced.

According to the lineage texts, the **Tiger** and **Rabbit** are not just powerful assets for each other, but they share a Zodiac house known as the *House of Growth & Development*.

This pair has can build something meaningful together. One creates, while the other manages the vision. One uses strength and takes action, and one uses diplomacy and strategy. So this is a perfect commercial partnership in which all kinds of hidden complementary talents will eventually surface. This is an auspicious relationship.

FENG SHUI ADVICE: It is a good idea to strengthen the Tiger presence in your life by placing the **image of the Tiger** in the Northeast 3 location. Better yet place a **Golden Deity** there as well. This activates the auspicious luck of the 24 Mountain star in the Tiger's location and can act as the catalyst for bringing you some excellent feng shui as well, especially if you are committed to each other.

The Rabbit's Astrological Enemy

Astrological feng shui relating to relationships and
compatibility between the twelve animal signs must
take note of one's "astrological enemy". Basically this is
represented by the animal sign that directly confronts
you on the Compass wheel.

In the case of the Rabbit, your enemy
is said to be the Rooster, and hence
communication between these two
signs is usually fraught with tension
& misunderstandings.

Whatever is going on between people born of these
two signs usually has an underlying hostile essence.
Very likely there is also very little in common between
these two signs; between siblings, two generations and
between relatives, this can be very trying and could even
lead to strong quarrels especailly if they live in the same
house.

Latent hostility and tensions rear their ugly heads...
unless there is also a Rat and a Horse, in which case the
family as a unit forms the *Four Elements Cardinal Cross*
of animal signs placed in the four primary directions.
North/South/East/West with Water/Fire/Wood/Metal
present!

151

This cross comprises the four elements which opens up the ability to engage the cosmic forces and hence this makes for a very auspicious phenomena existing within the family. Then whatever animosity there is is certain to transform into a potent combination of auspiciousness.

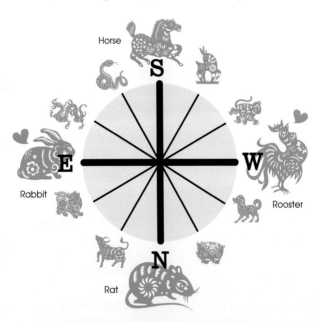

For the **Rabbit** in a relationship with a **Rooster**, if you also have a **Rat** and a **Horse** in your immediate family, this transforms the difficulties associated with being with your Zodiac enemy into very auspicious luck indeed.

PAIRINGS OF
ASTROLOGICAL ENEMIES

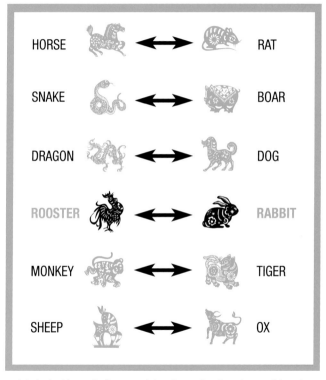

Astrological "enemies" can rarely be close unless there is something else
in the equation helping the union.

RABBIT WITH ROOSTER

Surprisingly cordial in a great year for this pair

The year 2012 brings exceptional good fortune to this pair who become incredibly formidable in what they can achieve especially if they are a pair, a team. This is a year when being cordial to each other enables them to reach new heights of great achievement indeed!

Despite them being astrological foes, this is a year when East can successfully meet West! These are two cardinal signs and ordinarily they are so diametrically opposite to each other that their friendship or relationship can be nothing more than superficial friends.

Going too deep will cause serious doubts and misgivings to surface. In the Chinese Zodiac the Rabbit and the Rooster are naturally hostile to each other and they will bring nothing but heartache to one another even though no such negative emotions were are ever intended.

From the way they think to the way they work, to how they analyse and respond to others, these two signs have vastly different styles and attitudes. The Rabbit occupies the East, the place of the rising Sun while the Rooster rules the West, the direction of the setting sun.

In terms of their attitudes therefore, one is naturally positive and hopeful, while the other tends to be morose and saturnine. The Rabbit is symptomatic of Spring when new shoots appear, so it signifies growth and enthusiasm. The Rooster is diametrically opposite representing the sober realities of the Fall season which heralds the coming of Winter.

So this pair cannot see eye-to-eye. If they try, they could well ignite some enthusiastic sparks between them, but when push comes to shove, someone is sure to get hurt. Note their elements are Wood for the Rabbit and Metal for the Rooster, so here Wood gets cut by Metal. This does not bode well for the Rabbit at all. Prospects look quite foreboding indeed.

But fuelled along by the positive energies of the year, it is not a bad idea to deepen and solidify the foundations for this relationship. Astrological indications can after all be subdued, especially when both sides wear powerful element amulets. So if you are already married and you started out in a special relationship with the Rooster, this is a great year to strengthen the relationship.

Another even better way is to bring amazing good fortune by having two children, one born in the year of the Horse and one born in the year of the Rat brought into the family. This creates what feng shui experts refer to as the cardinal cross. It is also referred to as the *Peach Blossom Cross*. This brings power and fame for the family and the balance that gets created is caused by the tension strings formed by these two pairs of "enemy signs" except that as a cross they indicate excellent good fortune.

And if you are in business together, use intermediaries to ensure you do not get too close to each other. Or add two key employees one born in the year of the Rat and the other in the year of the Horse.

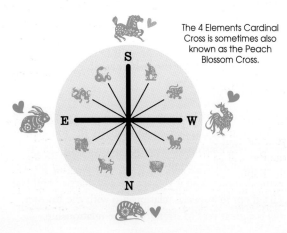

The 4 Elements Cardinal Cross is sometimes also known as the Peach Blossom Cross.

RABBIT WITH RAT

In 2012,
staying true despite distractions

The Rabbit gets along pretty well with the Rat, and in 2012, this makes a great love relationship. It is a strong pairing as both are amiable signs. The Rabbit will find it easy to enjoy good rapport with the Rat as its easy going nature and earth mother practicality comes across beneficial for the Rat.

In 2012, the Rabbit is strong and sure footed and this generates trust and excitement in the heart of the Rat sign. Also, in the Year of the Dragon, the personality traits of these two signs bode well for romance to either blossom afresh or if you are already in a love relationship, to find new levels of understanding and love. Between the two of you can flow a very beneficial partnership indeed. There is a good feeling of give and take, and the year's energy and its feng shui winds are very much favouring your friendship.

The Rabbit and Rat enjoy a happy convergence of goals; your thought processes are similar although, surprisingly, the Rat will be the more giving of the two. Happily, the Rabbit is not unappreciative, so compatibility vibes expand into good-natured tolerance and acceptance. The relationship is easy going and beneficial for both signs.

And since both can be equally focused and ambitious in outlook and aspirations, any coming together into some kind of partnership will be beneficial and cordial.

Both Rabbit and Rat are motivated by pretty similar goals, so as a couple, it is a partnership of equals. You can scale some new heights this year; and since the energies of the year favor you doing things together, any coming together of these two signs is beneficial.

It is however important to take note that there will be distractions that can come between you as a couple. The Rat needs to stay patient and should not give in to feelings of jealousy and resentment if Rabbit turns out to have a wandering eye. The effect of the peach blossom energy is very strong for the Rabbit, so those of you who are in a committed love relationship must be mindful of this.

The Rat needs to wear the amulet that prevents a third party coming in to stir things up between your relationship with the Rabbit. Stay watchful but also play it cool. Whatever distractions that crop up this year is likely to be short lived, so patience here is the name of the game. In any case, note that in a Rat-Rabbit pairing, it is the Rat who sustains the energy of the Rabbit.

The Rat's Water element fuels the strength of the Rabbit who in 2012 gets exhausted easily being afflicted by the *Reducing Energy Star* of the 24 mountains; what this means is that since Rat can give Rabbit good sustenance, any relationship between them is more than likely to stand the test of external distractions.

Note also that in 2012, it will be the younger of these two signs who will feel most acutely the highs and lows of relationship experiences. The year favors those friendships where the Rabbit is younger than Rat.

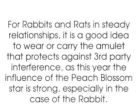

For Rabbits and Rats in steady relationships, it is a good idea to wear or carry the amulet that protects against 3rd party interference, as this year the influence of the Peach Blossom star is strong, especially in the case of the Rabbit.

RABBIT WITH OX

In 2012, excellent luck potential for this pair. They enjoy Ho Tu combination.

This pair usually do not have too much in common and usually there is also little to draw them together, but in the coming year of the Dragon, the Rabbit and the Ox are able to create an extraordinary kind of magic together.

HO TU GENERATES MAGIC: This is the year when the feng shui winds bring excellent energies their way and more, their numbers this year form the very auspicious Ho Tu combination. This translates into excellent good fortune for them both. They will generate quite an amazing synergy in whatever they do together, so there is potential for great happiness here.

Between them there is simply no tension at all and there are also no high expectations to create pressure of any kind on either of them. The Rabbit will benefit from the Ox feeling good about this relationship so a restful air of friendship gets created. The Rabbit enjoys something really deep with the Ox sign this year. In 2012 the Rabbit is feeling extra loving and romantic while Ox is satisfied with the way life is going. It is a good match indeed and they are both in a good place.

(*Excellent luck together this year* ★★★★)

Both signs exhibit a degree of compromise that makes it easy to decide on things, so all the major decisions that need to get made this year will be done in an atmosphere of love and great cordiality.

For the Rabbit, getting hitched to an Ox makes life less complicated than with some other signs. This is not to say that two are totally compatible. In fact, based on the Zodiac analysis, there are more differences than similarities between them; and on paper, they are not particularly well suited for each other.

There are differences in their life goals and personal aspirations; they like different kinds of people and they do not necessarily want the same thing in terms of career success or life goals. But the Ox finds the Rabbit's relationship vibes easy to live with and thus responds by showing a gentler side to its sometimes quite unbending nature.

It has to be said that the Ox sign is more down-to-earth than the Rabbit, who tends to have a weakness for luxury and a penchant for the glamorous life. The Ox is more of a workaholic bent on achieving things and making his/her mark in the world. So here we see two different kinds of energies that are not always moving to the same tune or in the same rhythm.

The Rabbit is also a lot more hang loose than the Ox. They dress differently, have different tastes in home decor and enjoy different hobbies. The Ox is a reader and loves the arts and classical music, and while the Rabbit can tag along as part of the whole relationship thing, this is not what turns the Rabbit on.

Despite these differences they will overlook everything in 2012. The two-year gap between them nevertheless sees the Rabbit giving in. The Ox benefits very much from this relationship.

The Ox who is in an important relationship with a Rabbit should carry the Ho Tu amulet to maximize the potential of the relationship.

RABBIT WITH DRAGON
In 2012, environmentally friendly couple stick together

The Rabbit should enjoy frolicking with anyone born in the year of the Dragon, and especially in a Dragon Year! This year favors both these signs, and although the Dragon has to put up with the five yellow afflictive star, nevertheless, getting together with the Rabbit should strengthen the Dragon's defences.

These two signs will enjoy **building a love nest** together simply because they have many things in common including their taste for luxurious things. This meeting of the minds creates a good foundation for them to get closer - and besides, both signs will find the latest trendy thing, being ecologically friendly to the environment, very easy to identify with.

Their ability to work together on the same cause should also fan the relationship further in 2012. The good thing about a Rabbit pairing up with a Dragon will be the relative serenity of this couple. There will be few if any loud words between them, and even though the Dragon is a rather domineering kind of person, the Rabbit has no problem taking this in its stride. In fact the Rabbit could find the Dragon's arrogance attractive. There is no problem here.

Nor will there be any seriously competitive vibes flowing between this pair. This is a very supportive relationship and there is also little danger of either looking outside the relationship to assuage either their ego or their libido.

This relationship does not get spoilt by petty egos clashing. The Rabbit has no problem creating a stable relationship with the Dragon as they are both able to see the big picture and instinctively work towards achieving results they both desire. These characteristics make an excellent basis to create something potentially sound and lasting together.

This goodwill arises from their connection to the season of Spring which forges a very special connectivity between these two signs. When it comes to forging a united front especially to deal with troublemakers or to withstand jealousy from outsiders, this pair has no difficulty in standing together. Their loyalty to each other is stable; thus they form a very special resilience which creates a great deal of happiness for them. The Dragon can fly as high or as far as he/she wishes, and the Rabbit is always around to offer support and a helping hand.

RABBIT WITH SNAKE

In 2012, hostile sparks fly, creating some problems

The Rabbit does not enjoy any special connectivity with the Snake. Both however are far sighted individuals whose intrinsic understanding of the chemistry of relationships cause them to interact in a mature fashion with one another, despite any absence of special rapport.

Rabbit and Snake will use their good nature and inherent wisdom to make their love or business relationships work, and because they can also be quite tenacious, they are likely to succeed.

These two are signs that can compromise and rationalise really well and they also tend to be resilient and determined in the way they approach their love life and their family situation.

Once committed, the Rabbit and Snake will work hard to make their relationship work. Here, wisdom and goodwill join forces to create a homely rapport which becomes a great foundation for long term stability. Except that in 2012, in the Dragon Year when transformational energies swirl around bringing unexpected distractions and temptations, sparks could

165

fly between the Rabbit and Snake pairing, bringing them either much closer together or flinging them far apart. It is wise to allow for the unexpected to happen in 2012 in this relationship.

The Rabbit has both a *Big Auspicious* and a *Yearly Conflict star* pulling it in two diametrically opposite directions, while Snake has stronger afflictive stars, the five yellow and the 3 killings, flanking it. These are signs of consternation that will disturb the calm of a solid and good relationship!

> **NOT AN EASY PAIRING:** Whether the relationship can withstand the unexpected depends on how deep a relationship they have. Theirs is not an easy pairing where understanding and trust comes easily. Actually, this pair does not trust each other much. The diplomatic Rabbit keeps its suspicions close to the chest, rarely revealing inner thoughts. The Snake too presents a totally detached face to the world.

So both are not people who reveal their feelings easily. So should this pair get into trouble in their relationship, their home becomes an acutely frosty place. Love will then have little place in the relationship, and the relationship could die. Even then it does not mean they will part company. No indeed. More likely they end up tolerating each other and leading separate lives, unable or unwilling to cause any disruption to the status quo. So, long term this might not be a happy couple – but it is not something very apparent to outsiders.

Having said this, theirs may not be a bad philosophy for living through troublesome years. Luck after all is cyclical and in terms their relationship, happy times are sure to roll by once again. In the meanwhile, other things can always engage their attention. Being practical people, the Rabbit and the Snake will survive very nicely no matter what.

The Rabbit and Snake are not a naturally compatible pairing, but with effort, it could work.

RABBIT WITH HORSE

In 2012, too much loving here, so need to cool things

These two cardinal signs can be in a mutually productive relationship, so the Rabbit and the Horse tend to be pretty cordial with each other. Both signs are well disposed to each other. There is admiration and respect, but usually from a distance rather than up close.

Should a relationship develop between this two, inner differences could surface leaving both sides to wonder if they really have anything in common at all.

The Rabbit being so down-to-earth and the Horse being such a free spirit. The Rabbit's attitude to life and living tends to be one of such unwavering stability where security and safety are carved in stone that the attitude of the Horse is sure to seem bohemian and irresponsible.

The Rabbit is often accused of living life in the bunker, never savoring the wind and rain and hidden from all the greater glory of the environment. At least this is how the Horse would respond to the Rabbit's well ordered life and values.

(*Hidden Tensions* ★ ★ ★)

The Horse after all has the call of the wild in its bones, a free soul spirit that is unwilling to be tamed. Adventurous and often foolhardy, the Horse stands for many things the Rabbit does not. One seems far braver and more of a risk taker than the other. So between this pair is a deep divide, so deep that should they live together or get married hidden tensions could very well surface.

In 2012 there is a great deal of love and tension in this relationship. The Horse's Fire energy excites and fuels Rabbit's interest and there is a need to cool things between this pair if they should move too fast. Too much loving here can cloud one's judgement...

The Rabbit should take note that life is one constant battle and the differences with the Horse can prove too fundamental to overcome so it is necessary to cool off. The differences between this pair can be quite insurmountable. In their journey through life, one cannot have a hundred percent trust that either will follow the other's lead. This becomes a big problem for them.

RABBIT WITH MONKEY

In 2012, not good for each other

This is an even more unstable pairing. The Rabbit and the Monkey do very little to benefit each other and any relationship between them is bound to be uneven.

Here, the Monkey could take charge completely leaving Rabbit feeling a little lost and definitely left out of whatever the Monkey is planning. Here, while both signs have great positive traits, what gets to come out in their interface will simply be so negative.

In 2012 they are definitely not good for each other! There is a basis for conflict to erupt in an ugly way. In any disagreement, the Rabbit will get hurt, so better NOT to get involved in a relationship here.

In this pairing, the Rabbit can get too mesmerized by the Monkey and this can be unhealthy, and it is advisable to walk away no matter how irresistible Monkey may seem. As long as Monkey stays faithful to the Rabbit, there should be no problem. But the problem is that the Monkey is a big flirt and in 2012, the Monkey is also strong and quarrelsome - not a good prospect for the Rabbit at all, because when the flirtatious Monkey starts to develop a roving eye, Rabbit stares potential heartbreak in the face.

Even when this couple are able to sustain a long-term relationship, it is only because of the tolerance and patience of the Rabbit, who will be the one giving in and swallowing whatever nonsense is being dished out by the Monkey.

So potentially, this is a pairing that does not bring any real happiness to the Rabbit. So no matter how debonair the Monkey appears, better in the long run to resist his/her charms and look elsewhere for long term commitments.

While Rabbit may fall for Monkey's charms, in the long term, this union is difficult to sustain.

Chapter Five

ANALYZING RABBIT'S LUCK FOR EACH MONTH IN 2012

The Rabbit quite a superb year this year and improves significantly from last year. You enjoy one star of Big Auspicious brought to you by the 24 mountains, coming from the Dragon side. This indicates that being close to Dragon born could bring a large amount of luck your way. Although you have the Reducing Energy star in your chart, your chi essence and health luck is generally good, so you are able to weather stress, and work under pressure if you have to. Relationships on the whole tend to go very well for the Rabbit this year; whether in work or play, you have a special knack of getting along well with others and can strike off a good rapport easily this year. Your best months fall in April, May, June, August, and January of 2013.

FIRST MONTH
February 4th - March 5th 2012

A NOISY & QUARRELSOME START CAUSES SOME TENSIONS

While you're embarking on an auspicious year, some remnants of insecurities linger from last year when some Rabbits may have undergone a stressful time. This month tends to be quarrelsome unless you can shed some of your hang-ups. Most of the obstacles you face are imagined ones, and if you can transform your mindset, you'll find life going a whole lot easier for you. Don't let yourself get stressed out so easily. If it helps, go away for a vacation, spend time to relax and unwind with the family… don't let yourself get sucked into an abyss of anxiety caused by imagined fears. Whatever you do, don't pick a fight. Learn to peace out and you'll get through the month a lot more happily.

WORK & CAREER - Keep Your Cool

This could be a testing month for the career Rabbit. Don't take your work too seriously. Be responsible but stay willing to see things from another perspective. Being obstinate and stubborn about things, no matter how much you believe in them, makes you difficult to work with as a team player and you could start to see

173

yourself being left out of the team. Keep a firm grip on your temper even if there are those who rile you; losing your cool could lead you to say or do something you'll regret massively later. If you are unhappy about something in your job, it is probably best to bite your tongue and live with it for now, at least until next month when the energies improve. Speaking out could get you into trouble of an unexpected kind.

BUSINESS - Proceed with Caution

There will be no shortage of opportunities coming your way, or good offers on the table, but it pays to proceed with caution this month. Beware of something that seems too good to be true, because it probably is. Put on hold grand ideas for later when your luck is stronger and more auspicious. This is a time when it is best not to jump into anything new, particularly waters that are unchartered. Stick with what you know best. You may meet with some disagreements and misunderstandings with business associates in the course of your work, but don't let isolated negative incidents blow out of proportion. Don't ruin a relationship you have spent time building up for something that's inconsequential in the long run. Giving your "wrong-doers" the benefit of the doubt is your best move this month.

LOVE & RELATIONSHIPS - Tension

There's a lot of tension in your relationships with others this month, particularly with those you know well. While Rabbits starting out in new relationships will have their honeymoon period, the next few weeks could prove quite noisy for those of you in a well-established relationship. Display six or more round, **smooth crystal balls** in the home to improve harmony within the marriage. Focus on being more understanding in your interactions with others.

Remember, it is not what is said or done that is remembered, but how make the other person feel. Loose words and careless actions on your part could have long lasting detrimental effects on whatever relationship you are working on, so for now, try and watch your words. Be mindful about what is said and done and you'll find both you and your partner are much happier for it.

 Avoid fixing engagements or wedding parties this month as the energies do not bode well for this for the Rabbit born.

SECOND MONTH
March 6th - April 4th 2012

ILLNESS AND A WEAK BODY TAKE THEIR TOLL ON YOU

Your main concern this month comes in the form of poor health and tiredness. Success and wealth luck is promising, and ventures commenced this month have a good chance of success. But while your work and professional life go well, you need to watch out for your health. You may suddenly develop a backache, or suffer from aches and pains. You are also more at risk of accidents, so it is best to be more careful this month. Make sure you get enough rest, don't work too many late nights and wear the **longevity symbol** near your body to keep up your personal chi strength. Older Rabbits should avoid sleeping in the East sector of their homes this month.

Older Rabbits should make use of the Longevity symbol this month. The illness star strikes, so if you are prone to sickness, it is vital to stay protected.

WORK & CAREER - Recognition

A promising time at work. If you can keep your mind focused on your work, you have a good chance of being noticed by all the right people. While you could face some unexpected competition, your confidence gets a boost from compliments given from the right quarters. Use that confidence to stay strong and to overcome your competition. The power of your mind is extremely powerful, so learn to use it to your advantage at this time.

BUSINESS - Socialize! Intereact!

This is an excellent month for Rabbits in business. Build on the relationship aspect of your work; you have outstanding people skills this month so make the most of this to widen your network, and to get to know those you work with better. The effectiveness of your communication is enhanced this month, and you can further activate this luck by wearing the **Fire Totem Talisman Pendant** near to your throat chakra. You make an effective boss and an exciting business partner, and everything you do involving other people this month allows you to shine. Don't shut yourself off from others at a time like this. You feed of the energies of other people, and the more you socialize and interact, the more energized you become. This will help you overcome the illness star that has flown into your chart.

LOVE & RELATIONSHIPS - Strength

This is a happy time for lovers and love may be just what the doctor ordered! A healthy relationship will keep some of you out of trouble, and will energize those of you feeling tired or burnt out. You have great support luck this month and for the married among you, you'll find a lot of that support coming from your better half.

The single Rabbit could get busy this month! This is a good time for dating, going steady, taking things to a new level and even getting married. The power of 2 is strong this month and favors the Rabbit doing things in a pair. You enter relationships with a renewed sense of love and compassion, and even old relationships are given the benefit of a breakthrough of sorts if the two of you are willing to try new things together.

FRIENDSHIPS - A Productive Time

This is a good month for the young Rabbit in school as long as you keep your energy levels up. You have the number 2 star in your chart which could sap some of your energy. Get your assignments done as soon as they are given to you to prevent stress becoming a factor. In general, a very productive month ahead.

THIRD MONTH
April 5th - May 5th 2012

COME SPRING TIME
AND YOU ARE REENERGISED

Your energy levels return and you are feeling rejuvenated and refreshed. This is a good time to start new things, turn over a new leaf, embark on new adventures. Two things in particular take center stage this month: your love life and your academic career. Those of you who are single and eligible will find romance and matters of the heart occupying most of their thoughts.

The young Rabbit will also do very well this month, and recognition and accolades are easy to come by. You're feeling motivated to do well, and the better you do, the more you are spurred on by the auspicious energies this month. Where the Rabbit needs to watch out this month are troublesome outsiders trying to enter the picture to disturb existing relationships. This applies to the married Rabbit in particular where there is danger of foolish infidelity. Married Rabbits are advised to wear the **amulet that protects against third party interference**.

WORK & CAREER - Inspiring Others

The working Rabbit will be kept very busy this month, with lots of existing projects to see through as well as new ones to start up. You may start to feel some pressure building up, but because you're feeling energized, you take on new challenges with gusto. In fact, the busier you keep yourself, the more productive you become.

The Rabbit is an ultra-efficient individual, and thrives on being very involved anything that in your mind matters. Those of you in managerial positions make inspiring leaders this month and have the ability to give real confidence to those you are leading. Go with your heart, hold firm to your convictions and enjoy the month.

BUSINESS - New Opportunities Open Up

Rabbits in business are in for a smooth ride this month. This is a good time to embark on new projects and ventures. Things you have been dreaming up can finally come to fruition without obstacles to slow you down. Go with the flow; it is much easier to let things fall into place than to try to fight the inevitable. Trust in your own good luck this month that things will work out for the best.

You may be approached with some exciting new opportunities and for some of you, this could be a major diversification from your main line of business. Go with your heart and go with your gut-feel. Your instincts are sharp this month and if you follow what you believe deep down, you won't make many bad decisions this month.

LOVE & RELATIONSHIPS - Riding High

Your love luck is riding high this month! If you are looking for something long term, there is every opportunity for you to find the right partner. Don't settle for second best. The right person will come along if you're patient.

If you've recently come out of a relationship, ensure you don't jump straight into a rebound relationship. But chances are you will meet someone really special by the end of the month. Be sociable this month. You're not going to meet anyone exciting just sitting at home. Accept those party invitations, or throw your own party! A great time for the Rabbit looking for love!

Married Rabbits however have to beware danger of infidelity. If your relationship is already patchy, you may have to put in extra effort this month to re-stabilize things. It is easy for a third party vulture to swoop in for the kill when external peach blossom energies come into the picture. But forewarned is fore-armed, and no one ought mess with a possessive Rabbit!

FORTH MONTH
May 6th - June 5th 2012

GOOD MONTH WHEN
EVERYTHING STARTS TO HAPPEN

A fabulous month indeed when you enjoy the blessings of the *Ho Tu*. This powerful combination promises the Rabbit person much success and recognition luck this month. The more you do, the more successful you will be. This is really the case where what gets put in comes out, so the more effort is expended on something, the better the outcome. You can rest easy that your efforts will not be in vain and whoever you are trying to please will indeed be delighted with your efforts. Those of you at a crossroads in your life will suddenly see things more clearly, and the direction you ought to take becomes much clearer.

WORK & CAREER - Winning Ways

Those of you in professions requiring you to perform, entertain or communicate will do especially well this month. Your oratory power gets enhanced and everything you say tends to be very well received.

You have an infectious sense of humor and everyone who interacts with you are immediately put at ease. Make use of your winning ways with people this month to cultivate and strengthen relationships. You could do with a few more allies at the workplace. Lunch with your colleagues, meet up with associates, make some cold calls... You can't go very far wrong right now, so don't waste this opportunity to make some giant strides in your career.

BUSINESS - Good Time for New Ventures
This month you may have to use your goodwill to further some causes close to your heart. Make the call, because chances are you will be doing whoever you are trying to get in touch with a favor as well. A good time to start new things and enter into new partnerships or joint ventures. When involving another party, think win-win. The more generous you are when striking a deal, the better the chances of success for the both of you. Don't look to outsmart anyone this month. You'll reap far more exciting rewards by working together.

LOVE & RELATIONSHIPS - Excitement
There is vigorous Fire energy in your chart this month, which indicates passion and adventurism re-surfacing in your life. Those of you who give way to your desires will

find this month a rollercoaster ride indeed. Whether this is a good or bad thing depends on where you are in your life, and whether you are single or attached. The single Rabbit will have no shortage of admirers, but going with the right one becomes more tricky. It is tempting to go with the dashing and dangerous, rather than the docile but dependable; even if the latter looks to probably make a much better long-term mate and less likely to break your heart.

While Rabbits traditionally like a bit of security in their lives, this month you seek out excitement. And if you're not in for the long haul and are just looking for a bit of fun, you can afford to test the waters a bit. Taking some risks could well lead you to an unforgettable joyride… and the bad boy or hot chick could turn out to be your fairytale romance that lasts and lasts.

EDUCATION - Taking On More
You're feeling full of energy this month, and with your liveliness and enthusiasm, you can afford to take on a lot without compromising quality in any one area. Keeping a good balance in life will also ensure your schoolwork stays enjoyable.

FIFTH MONTH
June 6th - July 6th 2012

ANOTHER THIRTY DAYS OF SHEER BRILLIANCE LIGHTING UP YOUR LIFE

The Rabbit is in for a fabulous month indeed! The number 8 star makes an appearance, bringing prosperity and riches of all manner into your life. Money comes easily and some of you may be in for a windfall of some kind. You're feeling creative and competent, and ideas you put forward are well received. Your personal life is just as satisfying as your work life and there's plenty to be happy about. Surround yourself with people who make you feel good about yourself; don't let one wet blanket spoil your fun. You have an auspiciously amazing time ahead and you don't need any killjoys in your life jeopardizing that.

WORK & CAREER - Recognition & Glory

This month sees you being given more responsibilities. You will relish being depended upon and this makes you perform like the star that you are. A fabulous month to expand your resources, increase capital and enhance capacity. Your have great talent which soon becomes obvious. Do enjoy yourself and bask in your well-deserved glory at work. You will find yourself in demand by those who value brains and talent. The good thing for you this month is that all this newfound praise and commendation inspires little jealousy. Even those who typically see you as a threat realize it is better to have you as an ally. Hang a **painting of a mountain** behind where you sit at work to ensure you maintain support on all fronts when it comes to your career.

BUSINESS - Fruitful Time for Networking
An auspicious time indeed for the Rabbit in business. Use your lucky stars to your advantage this month to close contracts and to bid for new projects. Your creative mind is working overtime to think up new ways to improve your business. This is a fruitful time to network and to be sociable, so accept invitations and overtures to interact with different and new people. They bring new ideas and fresh perspectives to your attention.

Those contemplating property-related investments can do so with courage and confidence as Earth luck is particularly good for the Rabbit this month.

LOVE & RELATIONSHIPS - Lucky in Love

You come to appreciate your partner a whole lot more this month. You're happiest in company, and if you are currently in a relationship, you start to realize how much you care for your partner. For some of you this may mean taking the next step forward. This is a lucky month for engagements and weddings, and those of you in this juncture of your relationship can commit with confidence.

For the single Rabbit, there is promise of meeting someone you feel you can truly connect with, not just at a physical level but a deep emotional one as well. Be courageous about committing; if you hesitate too long, you could lose something really good that makes its way into your life this month.

EDUCATION - Confident

The young Rabbit enjoys huge self assurance this month. You are up for trying new things and are great fun to be around. Your social life flourishes and you make new friends this month. While your extracurricular life becomes busier, you continue to do well in your schoolwork. On the whole and very happy month for the Rabbit child.

187

SIXTH MONTH
July 7th - Aug 7th 2012

MOVING SWIFTLY AHEAD BUT OVERCONFIDENCE CAN MAKE YOU CARELESS. BE CAREFUL.

The number 7 metallic star flies into your sector bringing danger of robbery, violence and being cheated. Be more careful when it comes to personal safety this month. Also be more careful when entering into agreements and new ventures in partnership. Not everything may be as it appears. It is easy for the Rabbit person to be fooled this month. Don't let yourself get taken for a ride by a smooth talker. If family or good friends sound a warning, take their advice seriously.

Not a good month to invest large amounts of money, as you're treading risky waters. Consolidate, philosophize, strategize. Or go away on holiday. Don't make big decisions this month. Carry the **Blue Rhino and Elephant talisman** to ward off danger from snatch thieves. Lady Rabbits should avoid venturing out too late at night by themselves. Always put safety first this month.

WORK & CAREER - Share Responsibilities

There is a lot going on at work, and it may seem that as soon as you complete a task, there is a new one to tackle. Exhaustion seems to overtake you regularly this month. It is worthwhile to take some time out to schedule your time better or you could suffer a collapse. Take it slower this month. Excessive work with no break does nothing for productivity and you could start making careless mistakes that could prove costly. Learn to work effectively in a team situation. Don't try to do everything yourself. You have to start trusting others. Allowing others to take on some of the responsibility will also make you a better manager.

BUSINESS - Don't Be Too Trusting

Do not be too trusting this month as you could be swindled. Keep a distance with new business associates and don't let on too much. There is also possibility of a dishonest insider in your midst. Make sure all checks are in place, and don't open yourself up to risk. When making decisions, be sure you have all the facts and information before deciding on anything. Make decisions based on your own findings rather than on the word of someone else, especially if you don't yet know them well. This is not a good month to sign new deals or enter into new areas of business. Put expansion plans on hold and keep the focus on your core business.

Also not a wise time to bring in new hires. Leave changes to working structure within your company to a later time. For the moment, maintaining the status quo is best plan.

LOVE & RELATIONSHIPS - Scandalous

There is danger of scandal when it comes to love and romance. Be careful when out partying, especially with new people. Don't mix business with pleasure too often. Especially if you are single, you are vulnerable to advances by inappropriate parties. And if you are married, all the more reason to be careful. This month it is not all about innocent love, but rather impassioned romance that could lead to embarrassment and even heartache after. Beware of your own actions and don't lead anybody on. Married Rabbits should quell the interference star with strong Earth energy or with the **Rooster with fan and amethyst**. This will protect against infidelity and the interference of a predatory third party.

Carry the Rooster with Amethyst and Fan to counter danger of infidelity this month.

SEVENTH MONTH
Aug 8th - Sept 7th 2012

SUM-OF-TEN MONTH BRINGING POSITIVE FINANCIAL & RELATIONSHIP LUCK

The stars in your chart form an extremely positive combination this month, bringing you luck from the heavens with an unseen helping hand in all that you do. You enjoy promising **wealth and prosperity luck**, as well as opportunities for new romances to blossom. Established relationships likewise can deepen this month if you make an effort to nurture them.

While things may be going very well for you, beware not to get overconfident, as this could spoil everything for you. When advice is given, accept it graciously. While you may not take up every morsel of advice offered to you, it is good to listen. Wisdom ripens in the strangest of forms and from the unlikeliest of sources. The less you think you know, the more you can successfully learn this month. Carry the **Heaven Talisman** to strengthen this aspect of your luck this month.

WORK & CAREER - Mentor Luck

This is a time to move resolutely forward and to go after what you want, even if there appears to be obstacles. Whatever difficulties you may face are temporary and surprisingly easy to overcome, as long as you are not fazed by them. You have heaven luck on your side, so trust in the divine to help you out of any sticky situation you may find yourself in. Relationship luck is excellent this month, so use the next few weeks to strengthen your friendships within your work environment. You also enjoy marvelous mentor luck. Those of you with a mentor figure in your life, and especially if he or she is directly involved in your work life, will find them a huge source of encouragement over the next few weeks.

BUSINESS - Exciting New Possibilities

Wealth and money luck are definitely on your side this month, which means that financially you are in a good position. Take fullest advantage of your good fortune luck this month. This is a lucky time to pursue new ventures and to go after opportunities that excite you. You are successful in all that you do; it is only a question of how successful. You can proceed with confidence and live life on the edge a little. Pursuing something you are really passionate about could unveil an exciting new niche for you.

LOVE & RELATIONSHIPS - Satisfying
Single Rabbits looking for love will have no problem
finding it this month. It is a fabulous time when it
comes to romance and a hugely satisfying one. Make
the most of your good form to go out there and
socialize. There is great depth to your conversations and
people find you incredibly interesting. Some will fall
hard for you; when more than one does is when it could
get complicated. Avoid any kind of love triangle because
someone will get badly hurt.

Married Rabbits will also enjoy the month with their
partners; it is easy to become closer as you find yourself
enjoying opening up to your partner more. They will
follow your cue and as a result, the two of you could
rediscover some of the magic lost over the years. A
great month for weddings, engagements and renewal of
marriage vows.

EDUCATION - Mentor Luck
This month the young Rabbit benefits tremendously
from the influence of a good mentor person in their life.
Make an effort to become closer to your teachers. If you
need help on something, don't hesitate to ask; in fact
this could be the perfect opportunity to become friends
with your teachers.

EIGHTH MONTH
Sept 8th - Oct 7th 2012

TROUBLES ON THE DOMESTIC FRONT OR IN YOUR LOVE LIFE

The misfortune star makes an appearance, making life difficult on all fronts, but particularly when it comes to relationships with the family or with your partner. Marriage squabbles become more common and small misunderstandings have the danger of blowing out of proportion. Try to stay calmer in the face of disagreements; this could save you a lot of aggravation. Carry the **"Ping" Peace Amulet** to calm down tempers, and the **Five Element Pagoda** to keep the five yellow star under control. When it comes to work and business, avoid taking risks this month. Not a good time to invest in anything new. Hold off any signings or launches till next month when your luck improves. Obstacles may arise making your life extremely difficult, and making tasks seemingly impossible to complete. But do persevere, because you will overcome whatever difficulty arises. You enjoy quite a fabulous year overall so don't let one bad month faze you.

WORK & CAREER - Keep a Low Profile

When it comes to work, this is a time to keep a low profile. Stay committed and continue to deliver good work, and take your responsibilities seriously. But don't try to make any moves that are too clever. Save your efforts to impress the boss for another time. Being too showy now could draw negative rather than positive reactions. Take note that when luck is not on your side, your speech has little power. So this is a time when it is advisable to keep quiet rather than speak out. Use this time to learn, collate information, and hone your skills. This is not the time to showcase anything.

BUSINESS - Put Plans on Hold

Big dreams and grand ideas should be put on hold. There is bad luck in your chart, so this is not the right time to undertake any kind of risky venture. Even when the venture is not a risk, things can still go wrong and obstacles come from unexpected quarters. Be conservative and detached. Those of you active in the stock market should be extra careful since this is a month of loss for you. Even if you think you are sure you know the market, resist the temptation to get involved. It is better to wait for a more opportune time than to jump into something that could get you stuck for some time.

LOVE & RELATIONSHIPS - Go Slow

Not an easy time for Rabbits in relationships. Small quarrels develop into full-blown tiffs, and if neither of you backs down, the disagreement grows larger and larger. Enough of these and it could be the straw that breaks the camel's back. If you are in a rocky marriage, this month there is real danger that things could fall completely apart unless you are aware of the risk, and take measures to counter it. Wear the **talisman** that protects the marriage from third party interference, and make an effort to be more understanding with your spouse. Engineer more time spent together, even a holiday away if you need.

Single Rabbits should probably wait till the month is over before pursuing any love interest with any kind of seriousness. Not a good month to take things to the next level. Better to go slow.

EDUCATION - A Little Tougher

Schoolwork is a little tougher and served out in larger quantities than usual, or at least that's how it seems. Start assignments as soon as they are set to avoid last-minute stress when submission deadlines come around.

NINTH MONTH
Oct 8th - Nov 6th 2012

TOO MUCH LOVING CAN CAUSE COSTLY DISTRACTIONS. STAY COOL.

The energies, both good and bad, are doubled this month, so it is particularly important to enhance the good aspects of your luck and to suppress the less fortunate aspects. Relationships in particular can get intense. If you use this to your advantage, you can sow the seeds of some lifelong friendships. On the other hand, relationships that are romantic in nature will have a tendency to get out of hand. Married Rabbits should be careful not to get swept away by a good-looking stranger if you spend long periods of time away from your spouse. Long distance relationships especially will come under strain. Even those of you in legitimate relationships could find them taking their toll, by being a great distraction, causing you to slacken when it comes to work or responsibilities. Watch your conduct when it comes to love. Strike a good balance in your life and don't overdo any one aspect.

WORK & CAREER - Temptations

There are romantic temptations at the workplace, where mixing business and pleasure becomes a real but

197

potentially hazardous possibility. If you find yourself attracted to someone at the office, the best thing to do is to strongly resist the temptation to form any kind of relationship that's not strictly professional, especially when it is your superior you have feelings for. Starting up something with your boss is asking for trouble. Do not play with fire. On a more positive note, you will find yourself more creative this month. You have the potential to do very well in your career, as long as you can keep your feelings and your conduct in check.

BUSINESS - Networking Brings Gains

This month is promising when it comes to building on relationships with the people you work with. Your relationship luck is excellent this month, so make it a point to interact extensively with others. Be seen around town. Rekindle old contacts. Form new ones. It is good for business and will do great things for your image at this time.

However, be careful of the romance star – it is over-activated this month, causing risk of illicit affairs. Keep control of yourself, do not over drink at parties, and maintain an old-fashioned morale. No good will come of being casual about relationships, and even innocent flirting can lead to scandalous disaster if you are not careful. Carry the talisman that protects against predatory third parties, and also maintain some self-control.

LOVE & RELATIONSHIPS - Too Hot

There is real danger of infidelity this month, particularly if you find your partner is not satisfying your needs for love and romance. But before you allow yourself to do anything foolish, do consider the repercussions and the long term significance. It is almost always better not to fool around, unless you have absolutely no desire to protect your current relationship. You're passionate this month and it will take little to throw caution to the winds. This makes you particularly vulnerable to indecent advances. Even if you are single, if you give in to your passionate nature this month is could be dangerous. Don't lose control of yourself, and don't put yourself in potentially dangerous situations.

EDUCATION - Focus

This is a very good month for the young student Rabbit. The academic star has flown into your sector, bringing you examination luck as well as making the learning process easy and enjoyable. This is a good time to put more attention to your studies and to focus. You are capable of making some serious breakthroughs this month.

TENTH MONTH
Nov 7th - Dec 6th 2012

HOSTILITY IN YOUR PERSONAL LIFE SPILLS OVER INTO YOUR WORK

The troublesome number 3 star returns, playing havoc with all your relationships. Some of you may have to deal with some upsetting incidences related to love and matters of the heart, and sometime work gets affected. Try not to let personal problems affect your effectiveness at the workplace because this also comes at the very inconvenient time when bonuses are decided and new promotions for the new year are being considered.

Watch also that you don't make enemies for no reason by being short-tempered or insensitive to others. Just because things may not all be going right for you does not mean you need to make everyone else's life a misery. If they are not close to you and in fact your direct contender for a promotion, they could well use it to their advantage to show you up in a bad light. Watch your words and your temper this month.

WORK & CAREER - Don't Lose Your Cool

It is important for you to weaken the quarrelsome star this month with Metal energy, or Fire energy. You can do this by wearing gold jewellery and the color red. Don't let problems in your personal life spill over into your work. Slacking when it comes to your job could not come at a worst time, so do put some energy into making sure you keep up the quality of your work. Those of you who work in competitive environments could find this a stressful time, with office politics to deal with. Stay calm and don't lose your cool, ever. Even when someone is trying to aggravate you on purpose, resist the temptation to react and to retaliate. Always give yourself a moment to think before acting. You're in danger of making some rash decisions that land you in hot water, so do be a bit careful on this front.

BUSINESS - Misunderstandings

Problems get created out of misunderstandings and there seems to be an underlying air of hostility with clients, business associates and customers. Some of you could even be slapped with a lawsuit if you are not careful. If this happens to you, do check your legal position carefully before responding to any hostile action towards you or your company. Reacting hastily might exacerbate an already bad situation. If it takes a small amount to settle a dispute, it is better to deal with it outside the courthouse.

LOVE & RELATIONSHIPS - Relax

Don't try too hard to impress anyone this month. It won't do you any good or win you any friends. This month is unfortunate when it comes to relationships of all kinds, but especially your love life. Any attempt at humor will fall flat, or worse, could come out sounding like an insult. Avoid friends who gossip and can't keep a secret. What you tell them with the best intentions can get twisted and stretched in the worst way possible. This month is better spent lying low and engaging in quiet solo activities like reading or jogging. Relationships that do best this month are those when you both give each other lots of space.

EDUCATION - Be a Model Student

Don't be a rebel this month or you're bound to be caught. Avoid breaking the rules, do your school work diligently and try to be the model student. While your parents may be the biggest nags, try to see the good side of things – they are only trying to help. Not the most satisfying of months for the young Rabbit, but at least year end is near and the Christmas break next month will give some respite.

ELEVENTH MONTH
Dec 7th - Jan 5th 2013

CHILL OUT THIS MONTH
TO ESCAPE THE SICKLY BLUES

The main thing you need to protect against this month is the afflicted energy from the visiting illness star. This is an Earth affliction and is best controlled by wearing a **Wu Lou** made of gold. You will tend to fall sick more easily and are more susceptible to viruses and bugs. Keep your immune system up by taking lots of vitamins and getting enough sleep. Overworking and stress could cause a minor illness to get quite bad quite quickly. Take it easy. It's the end of the year so try and relax a little. It will do you a world of good and also get you all refreshed for a brand new year.

WORK & CAREER - Keep Your Senses

While career luck is generally very good, you do run the risk of falling sick and thus jeopardize your ability t grab opportunities that come your way. So the important thing for the ambitious Rabbit is to not get overly ambitious. Relax a little and avoid overworking.

203

Look after your health and immune system. Don't skip meals and avoid too many late nights. You need to stay bright and alert in your interactions with the boss and with colleagues. For those of you attending end of year office parties, don't over indulge in drink. Keep your senses about you. Even though these parties are about having fun and bonding, you are being watched and a wrong move at one of these socials could overshadow good work you've been delivering all year.

BUSINESS - Take It Easy
Business luck is good. You may be presented with several irresistible opportunities this month, but it is best to wait till next month to act on them. The next four weeks are best spent planning and strategizing than on rolling out plans and getting things going. Use the month to focus on your core business and leave any possible diversifications of either products or methods till next month. It is not a stressful month for the Rabbit in business, so don't stress unnecessarily. Keep your immunity up, and leave the general running of things to your best man. You deserve a break once in a while and this is as good a time as any to take one.

LOVE & RELATIONSHIPS - Be Frivolous
This is a great time to spend with your partner building on your relationship with each other. Rabbits planning a

honeymoon-type getaway will enjoy themselves tremendously. This is a fabulous month for couples, whether you are newlyweds, long-married or just dating. Make an effort to be with each other.

Avoid heavy discussion about the state of the world and instead go for softer subjects in your conversation. Avoid pressing for a commitment, whether with family planning on how many children to have or the splitting of finances. This period, enjoy the more frivolous aspects of your relationship and just enjoy each other for who you are, without the day-to-day baggage that builds up.

EDUCATION - Find Time to Relax

Use this end-of-year period to recharge yourself for a brand new year ahead. You cannot work all year through, and children especially need time where they can take a complete break from school work, studies and responsibilities. Enjoy yourself this month. You're susceptible to falling sick this month, so don't live life too hard. Take it easy and learn to relax. Enjoy your friends. Indulge in hobbies. Or try a new extracurricular activity that takes your fancy.

205

TWELFTH MONTH
Jan 6th - Feb 3rd 2013

TIME TO BEGIN ANOTHER BRAND NEW YEAR

The new year begins especially well for the Rabbit. Your powers of persuasion are impressive and this month particularly refined. You can get just about anyone to come round to your way of thinking. For some of you, this skill of yours will come in handy indeed this month. You enjoy victory luck this month, giving you the edge in any competitive situation. Some of you will go through a transitional or transformational period when certain big changes take place in your life, but things work themselves out for the best. Even if there may be an adjustment period involved, you can be reassured that the stars are aligned very much in your favor this month. And even as you move away from this month and into the year of the Dragon, things continue to get better and better for you.

WORK & CAREER - Better & Better
Your professional life gets better and better over the next few months. You're getting along well with those you work with so turning up for work each day becomes

a joy rather than a chore. There is easy camaraderie between you and the rest of the team. You also make an excellent leader and those of you who get to showcase this talent will be impressive indeed. If you have ambitions to rise up to a high position within the firm you are working in, work towards it. You have all the luck in the world to achieve anything you would like to achieve. And the higher the aim, the more you will get. While you're likely to be showered with praise and appreciation this month, don't let yourself become big-headed. Success will come but stay humble if you want it to last.

BUSINESS - Close Deals On Your Terms
Rabbits in business could see offers on the table that are hard to refuse, but don't sell yourself cheap. Being too easy and giving in too much will only see you losing out in the long run. Drive a hard bargain to get the better end of the stick if you want the deal to work out. This is a month when you can move confidently forward with any plans you have. If there's a deal you want closed, by golly you will close it. But remember, on your terms. Don't be afraid to call the other party's bluff and be willing to walk away. You come from a position of strength and can afford to make that kind of a play.

LOVE & RELATIONSHIPS - External Romance

Single Rabbits will be in no shortage of suitors, and if your intention is to get hooked up with someone, this month could well see that happening. For those of you already in a steady relationship however, do watch out for interference from the outside. There could be outside interests vying for your attention and you can well be in danger of having your head turned. Married Rabbits especially ought to be more careful about this. The year boasts *External Flower of Romance luck*, and with your combination of stars this month, the external romance could become a reality. Both of you wearing the **Double Happiness symbol** will go a long way to protecting your union.

EDUCATION - Victory Luck

For the young Rabbit it is a carefree month where there is plenty of happy energy, which makes studying and school work a breeze. You find it easy to focus and your efforts should be reaping its rewards. For any of you thinking of applying for any scholarships or bursaries, luck is on your side and you can do so with some measure of confidence. Boost victory luck by displaying the **Victory Banner** on your workdesk, or in the East of your study room this month.

Chapter Six

PROTECTING YOUR TRINITY OF LUCK USING SPIRITUAL FENG SHUI

In recent years, the need to incorporate the vital Third Dimension into the practice of feng shui has become increasingly urgent - as we observe the unbalanced energies of the world erupt in earthquakes, giant tsunamis, volcanic explosions, fierce winds, snowstorms and raging forest fires. It seems as if the four elements of the cosmic environment which control the forces of Nature are taking turns to unleash their fearsome wrath on the world, in the process also generating fierce emotions of anger and desperation that elicit killing & violence.

Last year the threat of nuclear radiation poisoning the world's atmosphere, its winds and waters became for awhile a fearsome reality. The world watched as Japan suffered - it was a big wakeup call! Then came the hundreds of tornadoes unleashed on American States that destroyed towns and cities. Will 2012 see an end to Nature's wrath?

And what are the four elements of the cosmic environment? These are **fire** and **water**, **earth** and **wind**. These four elements signify the cosmic forces of the **Third Dimension in feng shui**; these forces are powerful but they are not caused by some evil being out to wreak revenge or death on the inhabitants of the world.

What they are, are highly visual manifestations of the severe imbalances of energy that need to be righted, and the process of rebalancing causes millions of litres of water to get displaced, hence the severe rainfalls and the tsunamis. They cause thousands of miles of earth to get shifted, hence earthquakes and volcanic eruptions, which in turn causes winds in the upper atmosphere and the currents of the seas to go awry. Temperatures blow very hot and very cold... and pockets of the world's population experience suffering, loss and depravation!

In 2010 and 2011, the onslaught of natural and manmade disasters befalling the world were reflected in the feng shui and destiny charts of those years, and the revelations of the charts of 2012 suggest a need to use spiritual feng shui to find solutions, seek safeguards and use protection to navigate through these turbulent years; to be prepared... so to speak.

In their great wisdom, the ancient Masters had somehow devised specific methods, rituals and almost magical ways to safely live through disastrous times. For of course these natural calamities have repeated themselves - in a series of cyclical patterns - over thousands of years.

We know that the world's energies work in repeating patterns and that there are cycles of change which affect our wellbeing.

To cope with these dangerous forces, it is necessary to decipher the charts, analyze the destructive forces revealed in the patterns of annual elements and then to apply cosmic remedies and transcendental cures - all part of the Third Dimension that completes our practice of feng shui. To enhance our trinity of luck i.e. our Heaven, Earth and Mankind luck.

In practicing spiritual feng shui, we look to generate good mankind luck, the luck we directly create for ourselves. The Buddhists and the Hindus call this luck generating good *KARMA*... and this is a concept that can be found in many of the world's spiritual practices.

Karma suggests that we can improve our luck, increase our longevity and experience happiness by purifying karmic debts and creating good merit through the practice of kindness, compassion and generosity. These are the basics. Thus we discovered through the years that our feng shui work and advice always worked best when we mindfully input genuinely kind motivations.

This led us to start using rituals of purification and appeasement to keep the four elements of fire, water, earth and wind balanced around our places of living and working. We discovered that there were direct correlations between the **four elements of the cosmic world** and the **five elements of the human world**.

Different animal signs are ruled by different elements at different times. Here we found that in **time dimension feng shui** - analyzing the annual and monthly charts to study the movement of element energy over time, spiritual methods played a big part in helping us improve our use of appeasement and purification rituals. They helped us to bridge the divide between the cosmic worlds - the spiritual worlds that existed alongside ours, and to add so much to our practice of feng shui. Included in the practice of Third Dimension spiritual feng shui are rituals and vocal incantations that can quell imbalances of energy.

There are powerful prayers and special offerings that can be used to invoke the aid of the cosmic beings of our space, the local landlords who rule our environment; the spirits and protectors who can assist us subdue the angry earth, control the raging waters, and basically keep us safe, making sure we will not be in the wrong place at the wrong time, that somehow we will change our plans, delay our travels or just stay home during crucial times when the elements of the world will be out of sync and raging.

Spiritual feng shui brings the practice of feng shui into other realms of existence. It addresses parallel world(s) that exist alongside ours; cosmic worlds inhabited by beings we call Spirits, local Landlords, protectors or even Deities who have supremacy over the elements.

> There are **Earth Deities** and **Wind Deities**, **Water and Fire Gods** - in the old lineage texts of the ancient masters, references are made to the **Four Direction Guardians**, the heavenly kings who protect the four directions, North, South, East and West corners of our world, of the **Eight Direction Goddesses** who subdue destructive forces of wind and water and protect mankind.

Much of the information related to these powerful cosmic deities has become the stuff of legends, but they are real; and it is not difficult to invoke the assistance of these cosmic beings. It would be a big mistake to dismiss them as mere superstition!

Included here are some of the easier methods of spiritual feng shui which just about anyone can indulge in without compromising your belief systems. Always perform these practices with good motivation which is to keep your family safe, and your life humming along without success blocking obstacles.

You will notice that the use of symbolism activated by the mind's concentrated power is extremely potent, as are the purifying and offering rituals. One of the most effective way of staying safe and secure in your world is to make and wear special **magic diagrams** that incorporate **sacred symbols** and incantations or **mantras** into what we collectively refer to as amulets.

This practice is usually referred to as *transcendental feng shui* and the methods are shamanic, totally magical in their effect. The amulet can be customized to benefit different animal signs directly, incorporating the energizing symbols and syllables most beneficial to their elements in any given year. The amulet for the Rabbit is given in this chapter here.

Spiritual feng shui also involves identifying the **special Deity** who has the greatest affinity with specific animal signs - these can be viewed as your **Guardian Bodhisattva**, similar to the patron saint or spiritual guide of each animal sign.

When you invite your **Guardian Bodhisattva** into **your** home, make offerings and recite their relevant mantra, you will benefit from the full force of their protective power. They will not only ensure that you stay safe and protected but will also multiply the potency of your time and space feng shui updates as well.

Incense Offerings to Appease Local Guardian Spirits

Everyone benefits from learning how to make incense offerings on a regular basis to communicate directly with the "local landlords" that reside alongside us in our home space, on our street, in our town or village or sometimes on separate floors of high rise buildings. There is no need to be scared of them or to fear them. Most will leave human tenants alone.

When incense is offered to them, it creates the element of gratitude on their part; that is when they could assist you in whatever requests you make. It is not a widely

Offering incense is one of the best ways to appease the local spirits of the land.

known fact, but Spirit Beings of the cosmic realm are always hungry, and at their lowest levels, they are known as hungry ghosts. The problem is that they are unable to eat!

They cannot swallow food as their necks are said to be extremely narrow and the only way they can appease their hunger is by smelling aromatic, pungent incense which is yummy to them.

But just burning the incense alone is not as effective as reciting 21 times the blessing incantation that transforms the incense into sustenance for them, and then it is like giving them a feast, and the stronger the scent is, the tastier it will be to them.

There are so many auspicious benefits to preparing and then burning this incense offering in the outside space of your home, and also in the inside space by moving round each room three times in a clockwise direction. Done once a week on your *Day of Obstacles*, the incense will chase out all negativities and cleanse your home of bad energy. The local spirits will then also attract success, good health and wellbeing. Whatever disharmony there is in the home will quickly dissolve and all the afflictions of the year will also dissipate.

For the Rabbit person, the best day to perform this incense offering ritual is **every Friday** and the best time would be to do it anytime **between 5pm & 7pm** in the afternoon.

In the old days, practitioners of this ritual would burn freshly-cut juniper on hot charcoal and this gives off a very pleasant aroma together with white smoke which is also very pleasing to the spirits. This method continues to be used by the mountain people such as the *Sherpas* of the Himalayan mountain regions. In fact, if you go trekking in Nepal, you will see all along the trekking routes examples of these incense offering rituals which are done to appease the local protectors hence keeping both visiting trekkers as well as the local people safe.

It is said that the more undeveloped a place is, the greater the presence of local spirits. Mountainous places are great favorites with the beings of the cosmic world. This is why those who go mountain climbing should always wear amulets to keep them safe from being harmed by some naughty wandering spirits.

Today however, especially if you live in the city, it is more convenient to use specially formulated incense pellets which burn easily and which give off a beautiful pungent aroma. The Malays and the Indians in Malaysia call this *kemenyen* and the Chinese sometimes use sandalwood incense powder to achieve the same effect.

Use a special incense burner that comes with a handle and as you light the incense recite prayers that consecrate the incense so that it becomes easier for the spirits to enjoy the offering incense. Remember to take a humble attitude when making the offering and if you are a Buddhist, you can also take refuge in the triple gems before you start. The incantation mantra, to be recited at least 21 times is:

NAMAH SARVA TATHAGATA
AVALOKITE OM SAMBHARA
SAMBHARA HUNG

Then think that you are making offering of the incense to the landlords and protectors of your house, your street and your neighborhood. You can think that they are accepting the incense and then you can request for specific illnesses or obstacles to be removed.

Those born in the year of the Rabbit can request for protection against any conflicts arising from neighbors or colleagues through the year.

Customized Amulets to Add to Rabbit's Strong Success Elements in 2012

There is a group of 102 Protective Amulets, reportedly first made in the **Tibetan Nyingma** monastery of *Samye*, the monastery in Tibet founded by the powerful **Tibetan Lotus Born Buddha** known as **Guru Padmasambhava** or **Guru Rinpoche** that is designed according to astrological calculations using the Chinese calendar i.e. based on the 60 year cycle of 12 animal signs and 5 elements.

Feng shui astrology attributes different influences arising from the different combinations that occur between the 12 animals and the 5 elements each year; these combinations of influences reveal the nuances of good and bad luck according to the year of birth.

Each sign requires different *sanskrit* syllables, symbols and invocations, which are meant to subdue bad influences facing the sign.

The amulet that is customized to
the animal sign also simultaneously
promotes all-round good influences
to come your way; it protects your
property, business & work interests,
and your family & your loved ones.

Worn close to the body or placed near you near you,
it increases your prosperity and keeps you safe from
wandering spirits, which you might inadvertently
encounter.

Amulet of the Wood Element

The Rabbit benefits from wearing what is referred to
as the Wood amulet; and it is shared with the other
"Wood sign" of the Zodiac, the Tiger. The amulet
is usually drawn as a circle and it incorporates the
empowering *Dependent Arising* mantra. The outermost
circle is embellished with patterns that symbolize
Wood and Water.

The Rabbit belongs to the Wood element, so Water
energy will strengthen Rabbit's intrinsic element and
in 2012, it is extremely beneficial to wear this amulet.
It should be written in red cinnamon ink and on dark
red or yellow paper or silk and then folded, then kept
in a suitable casing and then worn near to the body.

221

The Rabbit person benefits from wearing the Wood amulet,
which can block off adverse forces and keep planetary
afflictions subdued for the Rabbit.

Worn touching the body especially if the amulet has
been suitably consecrated, it can block off all adverse
forces, and keep all planetary afflictions subdued. The
amulet for the Rabbit can be made of rice paper or silk
and then kept inside a leather or metal pouch. In 2012,
the Metal element signifies power and influence so
having a gold or silver casing is appropriate.

We have also incorporated other powerful wish fulfilling amulets into silk neck scarves that can be worn around the neck, and these are suitable for dressing up your outfit while helping to actualize your wishes for you at the same time. Most amulets have a series of three concentric circles of mantras with a special syllable or symbol in the centre.

The Rabbit can wear these auspicious **wishfulfilling amulets** in 2012 and also those with the mantra of the **Goddess Tara** or with the special mantra that fulfils all wishes:

OM HANU PASHA BHARA HEH
YEH SO HA

And because Rabbit enjoys the luck of the peach blossom and intellectual pursuits, it is extremely beneficial for Rabbit to cement this year's good fortune vibes by inviting a **wish fulfilling jewel** into the home as well.

Clear Crystal Ball with Gold Ru Yi inside to Bring Rabbit to a New Power Level in 2012

The Rabbit sign has a good fortune star in 2012 bu it also has the *Reducing Energy Star* in its 24 Mountain Compass location; hence Rabbit benefits from anything that can strengthen its power and authority luck.

223

Golden Wealth Wheel Powerful Symbol of Upward Mobility for the Rabbit

The Golden Power Wheel can help the Rabbit activate its promotion luck and having it near your place of work will enhance your chances of promotion. Display the spinning wealth wheel which is created from two circular brass plates that are inscribed with the powerful mandalas of the male and female wealth Gods of the cosmic traditions.

Each side has eight images within the eight petals of a stylised lotus. These images of wealth gods and goddesses are placed facing each other, and when the plates are turned, the energy released from the wealth Deities being pleased, attracts wealth and prosperity into the home or office. At the back of the Male deities will be the eight auspicious signs and in the centre the seed syllable *Hum*; behind the female deities are the royal emblems and in the centre the seed syllable *Hrih*.

Do take note that this is a sacred representation of the Wealth deities, so they also bring wealth luck. It is an excellent idea to spin this **Golden Wealth Wheel** at least once a day. Do place the wheel on a high level i.e. on a sideboard rather than on a low coffee table.

Blue Dragon to Activate Rabbit's Sum-of-Ten Heaven Luck

The presence of the Dragon image will strongly enhance the *Rabbit's Seasonal Luck of Spring,* and in 2012 with the lap chun present and it being the Dragon Year displaying the image of the Blue Dragon attracts good fortune. In any case, because it is a Dragon Year, everyone benefits from the Blue Dragon image, but more so those born in the sign of the Rabbit. Place it in the East part of the living room or dining area.

Displaying the Blue Dragon in the East part of the living room will enhance the Seasonal Luck of Spring for the Rabbit-born.

Fire Totem Talisman Pendant to Safeguard Your Longterm Luck

One of the most popular ways of wearing several auspicious cosmic symbols together is to use the totem concept which groups three or more powerful instruments or symbols stacked one on top of another. Totems make powerful talismans when they are correctly made and properly energized with special incantations.

Cosmic totems that put together element groups of protective sacred symbols can be excellent for compensating for a vital missing element. In 2012, the Fire element signified by the color red is required to bring about a proper balance to the energies of the world; but more than that, 2012 is the kind of year when it is extremely beneficial to invoke the powerful **Bodhisattva** and **Deity Guardians of the Earth**, many of whom are associated with *sanskrit* syllables.

The Fire Totem Pendant comprises three powerful sanskrit syllables - at the base is *Bam*, followed by *Ah*, and then *Hrih* at the top. These syllables are strongly associated with the Tibetan spiritual traditions and the shamans of pre-Buddhist Tibet wear these syllables to keep them safe and empowered at all times.

But these syllables are also used as wish-granting aids in powerful spiritual visualisations.

The syllable *Hrih* is a very powerful symbol which protects and also sends out a great deal of loving energy. It makes the wearer appear softer, warmer and kinder.

The Fire Totem Talisman is a pendant made completely of gold which can be worn touching the throat chakra. Not many know it, but the throat chakra is red in color and it governs the power of one's speech. Anyone wanting their spoken words, their speech, their selling proposals and so on to become empowered can wear this totem pendant.

If you work in a profession where the way you talk, give a speech, make a proposal and otherwise use your voice is crucial, then this totem pendant is ideal for you. Those in the teaching profession, in law and in the entertainment industry, for instance, would benefit greatly from wearing it.

There is a lotus and an utpala flower joining these seed syllables - and all the five items in the totem are related to the Fire energy of red. The color red signifies the **Fire element**. The lotus signifies purity and the utpala flower suggests the attainment of great wisdom. This is a very powerful emblem not just for protection but more importantly for empowerment. When you wear them, think that they exude rays of red light radiating outwards from you in all directions.

Invoking Rabbit's Guardian Bodhisattva Manjushuri

The Rabbit's Bodhisattva Guardian is **Manjushuri** who is the **Buddha of Wisdom**. This is the Buddha one invokes to have good feng shui in the home and also to enhance one's knowledge of feng shui and other divination practices.

Manjushuri's presence in any home or work space brings sacred energy that increases your esoteric knowledge and your wisdom and is thus most beneficial. Look for an image that "speaks" to you and then invite the image into your home. Just having Manjushuri's presence in the home brings enormous good karma especially if placed in the East, the Rabbit's home location.

Place offerings of water bowls, candles and **food** to establish a "connection" and each time you make incense offering to the local landlords and environmental spirits, do include your Buddha Manjushuri by name in your list of recipients. It is a good idea to make the dedication to the Buddha first.

This need not be a very elaborate ritual. The key to success in incorporating spiritual feng shui into your daily life is to be very relaxed and joyous about all that you do. What is so beneficial about having your **Guardian Deity** in your home is that the spirits of the cosmic world always respect the Bodhisattvas and Buddhas and when you invoke their protection, it offers you safe refuge from being harmed by the spirits that may be residing in your space.

So What Do You Think?

We hope you enjoyed this book and gained some meaningful insights about your own personal horoscope and animal sign. This book, if used properly and regularly, is a goldmine of feng shui knowledge… so hopefully you are already feeling a difference and enjoying the results of positive actions you have taken.

But Don't Stop Now!

You can receive the latest weekly news and even more feng shui updates from Lillian herself absolutely FREE! Learn even more of her secrets and open your mind to the deeper possibilities of feng shui today.

Lillian Too's FREE online weekly ezine is now AVAILABLE!

Here's how easy it is to subscribe. Just go online to: *www.lilliantoomandalaezine.com* and sign up today!

Your newsletter will be delivered automatically
to your inbox each week
....

You will receive a special FREE BONUS from Lillian when
you subscribe to Lillian's FREE Mandala Weekly Ezine…
but it's only available to those who register online at:
www.lilliantoomandalaezine.com
....

Once you register for the weekly newsletter,
you become eligible for special discounts and offers only
available to ezine subscribers!
....

DON'T BE LEFT OUT! JOIN TODAY!

Thanks again for investing in yourself and in this book.
Now join me online every week and learn how easy it really
is to make good feng shui a way of life!

Lillian's online FREE weekly ezine is only available when
you register online at *www.lilliantoomandalaezine.com*